Best Climbs
Phoenix, Arizona

FALCONGUIDES®

An imprint of Globe Pequot
Falcon and FalconGuides are registered trademarks and Make Adventure Your Story
is a trademark of Rowman & Littlefield.

Distributed by NATIONAL BOOK NETWORK

Photos by Stewart Green unless otherwise noted.
Maps: Sue Murray © Rowman & Littlefield

British Library Cataloguing-in-Publication Information Available

Library of Congress Cataloging-in-Publication data available

ISBN 978-1-4930-2223-6 (paperback)
ISBN 978-1-4930-2224-3 (e-book)

♾™ The paper used in this publication meets the minimum requirements of
American National Standard for Information Sciences—Permanence of Paper for
Printed Library Materials, ANSI/NISO Z39.48-1992.

WARNING

Climbing is a sport where you may be seriously injured or die. Read this before you use this book.

This guidebook is a compilation of unverified information gathered from many different climbers. The author cannot ensure the accuracy of any of the information in this book, including the topos and route descriptions, the difficulty ratings, and the protection ratings. These may be incorrect or misleading, as ratings of climbing difficulty and danger are always subjective and depend on the physical characteristics (for example, height), experience, technical ability, confidence, and physical fitness of the climber who supplied the rating. Additionally, climbers who achieve first ascents sometimes underrate the difficulty or danger of the climbing route. Therefore, be warned that you must exercise your own judgment on where a climbing route goes, its difficulty, and your ability to safely protect yourself from the risks of rock climbing. Examples of some of these risks are: falling due to technical difficulty or due to natural hazards such as holds breaking, falling rock, climbing equipment dropped by other climbers, hazards of weather and lightning, your own equipment failure, and failure or absence of fixed protection.

You should not depend on any information gleaned from this book for your personal safety; your safety depends on your own good judgment, based on experience and a realistic assessment of your climbing ability. If you have any doubt as to your ability to safely climb a route described in this book, do not attempt it.

The following are some ways to make your use of this book safer:

1. Consultation: You should consult with other climbers about the difficulty and danger of a particular climb prior to attempting it. Most local climbers are glad to give advice on routes in their area; we suggest that you contact locals to confirm ratings and safety of particular routes and to obtain firsthand information about a route chosen from this book.

2. Instruction: Most climbing areas have local climbing instructors and guides available. We recommend that you engage an instructor or guide to learn safety techniques and to become familiar with the routes and hazards of the areas described in this book. Even after you are proficient in climbing safely, occasional use of a guide is a safe way to raise your climbing standard and learn advanced techniques.

3. Fixed Protection: Some of the routes in this book may use bolts and pitons that are permanently placed in the rock. Because of variances in the manner of placement, weathering, metal fatigue, the quality of the metal used, and many other factors, these fixed protection pieces should always be considered suspect and should always be backed up by equipment that you place yourself. Never depend on a single piece of fixed protection for your safety, because you never can tell whether it will hold weight. In some cases, fixed protection may have been removed or is now missing. However, climbers should not always add new pieces of protection unless existing protection is faulty. Existing protection can be tested by an experienced climber and its strength determined. Climbers are strongly encouraged not to add bolts and drilled pitons to a route. They need to climb the route in the style of the first ascent party (or better) or choose a route within their ability—a route to which they do not have to add additional fixed anchors.

Be aware of the following specific potential hazards that could arise in using this book:

1. Incorrect Descriptions of Routes: If you climb a route and you have a doubt as to where it goes, you should not continue unless you are sure that you can go that way safely. Route descriptions and topos in this book could be inaccurate or misleading.

2. Incorrect Difficulty Rating: A route might be more difficult than the rating indicates. Do not be lulled into a false sense of security by the difficulty rating.

3. Incorrect Protection Rating: If you climb a route and you are unable to arrange adequate protection from the risk of falling through the use of fixed pitons or bolts and by placing your own protection devices, do not assume that there is adequate protection available higher just because the route protection rating indicates the route does not have an X or an R rating. Every route is potentially an X (a fall may be deadly), due to the inherent hazards of climbing—including, for example, failure or absence of fixed protection, your own equipment's failure, or improper use of climbing equipment.

There are no warranties, whether expressed or implied, that this guidebook is accurate or that the information contained in it is reliable. There are no warranties of fitness for a particular purpose or that this guide is merchantable. Your use of this book indicates your assumption of the risk that it may contain errors and is an acknowledgment of your own sole responsibility for your climbing safety.

your safety depends on
your own good judgment,
based on experience and
a realistic assessment of
your climbing ability

Overview

Contents

Introduction

Phoenix, the sixth most populous city in the United States, offers climbers a wide selection of varied adventures on cliffs and crags scattered across its numerous mountain ranges. The routes range from scrambles up cliffs at Camelback Mountain, stiff crack climbs at Pinnacle Peak and in the McDowell Mountains, multi-pitch routes up pinnacles and buttresses in the Superstition Mountains, and excellent sport climbing at Queen Creek Canyon. The Phoenix area offers some of America's best winter climbing areas, with warm, sunny days in the depths of January. Besides the described climbing areas close to the city, area climbers head out to more distant sport climbing areas like The Homestead and Jack's Canyon (which are not covered in this book of best local climbs).

Climbing Seasons

Phoenix is hot during the summer months, making winter the ideal climbing season. The best climbing weather occurs from October through April, although expect some hot days during the shoulder months. Winter offers great weather for climbing, especially when snow plasters the rest of the United States. Some winter days might be too cold for comfortable climbing on shady cliffs, but shorts and a T-shirt are the norm for December cragging.

Summers are just too hot for comfortable climbing, even in the shade. Stay out of the sun on hot days, wear a hat, and carry plenty of water—a gallon per person is not too much. Drink Gatorade or other sports drinks to keep electrolytes and other essentials replenished.

If you are climbing in the heat of the day, you may not only get dehydrated but also develop heat-related illnesses, including heat cramps, heat exhaustion, and heat stroke—a potentially fatal condition. Heat-related illnesses are preventable by being smart, staying cool, and treating dehydration symptoms and overheating by drinking plenty of liquids and finding shade. Remember to drink a lot and often.

Land Management and Closures

All the described Phoenix climbing areas are on public lands, managed by the City of Phoenix, City of Scottsdale, and Arizona State Parks. Few restrictions exist at the climbing areas, allowing rock climbers to enjoy access and climbing freedom.

The McDowell Mountains and Little Granite Mountain areas are in Scottsdale's McDowell Sonoran Preserve. These areas as well as the city's

A climber rappels off the Praying Monk, one of the most popular climbing routes on Camelback Mountain.

Brian Shelton climbs Last Light up a steep slab on Rock Knob on the northern edge of the McDowell Mountains.

Pinnacle Peak Park have climbing guidelines about where climbing is allowed, accessing climbing sectors, and the placement and maintenance of fixed anchors.

The big problem at Camelback Mountain's Echo Canyon Recreation Area is parking. The mountain is often busy with hikers so the parking areas fill up quickly, especially in morning and evening. Time your visit for less busy times of the day and carpool to the area.

The main wildlife closure on Phoenix cliffs is on the North Face of Tom's Thumb in the McDowell Mountains. In the past, climbers have been asked to respect nesting raptors on the face, but the possibility exists that the cliff will be closed in the future. Check information on kiosks at the Tom's Thumb Trailhead for updated information on wildlife closures.

Climbing Rack and Extras

While gear suggestions are included in many route descriptions, what you carry on your climbing rack is up to you. Look at your proposed route and decide what you need to safely protect yourself when you climb. Make sure you bring enough gear—remember, the sin is never carrying too much gear, but not enough.

For traditional routes you may need a full rack of gear. A basic rack should include two sets of TCUs and cams to fist-size, one to two sets of wired nuts like Stoppers, ten to twelve slings with extra carabiners, and at least a dozen quickdraws. Some climbs require multiple same-size cams as well as off-width pieces like extra-large cams and Big Bros. Bring two 200-foot (60-meter) ropes for climbing and rappelling, although 165-foot (50-meter) ropes work fine. Also bring and wear a helmet. Loose rock abounds on the volcanic and granite cliffs, and a helmet can save your head and life.

If you're climbing in remote areas, bring extra webbing and a knife to cut it for replacing old slings on rappel anchors. Webbing wears out quickly in the harsh sun and heat. Bring plenty of water, either in bottles or a hydration pack. Gatorade or other liquids that replace electrolytes are essential for hydration in the heat. Wear sturdy boots or approach shoes for hiking across the spiny desert to your route. Bring a headlamp so you can see if you're benighted on a climb or on the hike out. A small GPS unit can keep you found in the desert, and a cell phone is a lifesaver in an emergency.

Climbing Dangers and Safety

Rock climbing is dangerous. That's a fact. The perils of climbing, however, are usually overstated. The risks we take are the ones we choose to take. Everything we do as climbers, including placing gear, setting anchors, tying into the rope, and belaying, is to mitigate the dire effects of gravity and to minimize the danger of climbing. It's up to you to be safe when you're climbing. Be safety conscious and use the buddy system to double-check your partner and yourself.

Redundancy is the key to your personal safety. Always back up every important piece of gear with another and use more than one anchor at belay and rappel stations. Your life depends on it. Beginner climbers are most vulnerable to accidents. If you're inexperienced, hire a guide or take lessons. Always use sound judgment when climbing and respect the danger. Don't attempt climbs beyond your ability and experience. Remember that most accidents happen because of climber error.

Objective dangers, as at most climbing areas, abound on the desert cliffs and towers around Phoenix. Pay attention to these dangers for a safe climbing adventure:

- Watch out for loose rock as you climb or if another party is climbing above. Loose flakes and boulders are commonly found.
- Wear a helmet to mitigate head injuries when climbing and belaying.
- Use any fixed gear with caution. Some climbs still have old pitons and bolts, and it's hard to determine how solid they actually are. Weathering and erosion weakens fixed pitons and bolts. Always back up fixed gear with your own.
- Rattlesnakes, found at all the climbing areas, can be a serious hazard during warmer months. Watch for snakes while scrambling to cliff bases, along access trails, and hiding under boulders and dead brush.
- Aggressive Africanized honeybees are found throughout the Phoenix area on cliffs, especially at Camelback Mountain. Avoid climbing routes with bee activity, including bees humming.

Use the following ten tips to stay safe when you're out climbing on the cliffs around Phoenix:

- Always check your harness.
- Always check knots.
- Always wear a helmet.
- Always check the rope and belay device.
- Always use a long rope.
- Always pay attention.
- Always bring enough gear.
- Always lead with the rope over your leg.
- Always properly clip the rope into carabiners.
- Always use safe and redundant anchors.

Martha Morris boulders
along the scenic Apache Trail
northeast of Phoenix.

Killer Bees Attack Arizona Climbers:
How to Avoid Swarms of Africanized Bees

On Friday, September 11, 2010, an Arizona man in his 50s was scrambling on 2,704-foot Camelback Mountain in Phoenix when he disturbed a hive of killer bees. Trying to get away, the man became stranded on a high cliff and was stung over 120 times while waiting for help. The Phoenix Fire Department worked for three and a half hours to rescue the man before lifting him to safety.

Camelback Mountain, an easily accessible landmark peak towering over Phoenix and Scottsdale, is a popular hiking spot with trails up both the east ridge and jumbled west flank of the mountain. The northwest side of the peak offers red walls of Tertiary-age mud and conglomerate, including the Praying Monk, a freestanding pinnacle and one of the most famous rock climbs around Phoenix.

This is not the first time climbers and scramblers have been attacked by Africanized honeybees on Camelback Mountain. One of the worst bee attacks occurred on March 7, 2004, when Keith Abbe and Jeff Passage were climbing the Hart Route, a fun and easy three-pitch line up the Gargoyle Wall above the Praying Monk. The climbers, belaying on a ledge below the last pitch, were attacked by a swarm of Africanized honeybees that had a hive 30 feet up a gully above the ledge. The climbers attempted to flee the bees. Abbe unroped and tried to descend but ended up falling 50 feet and was killed, the first known American rock climber whose death was the result of bees. Passage was stung over one hundred times but survived.

On Monday, October 29, 2012, three young men decided to climb unroped up the George Route, a classic easy route (4th class) on the north side of Camelback Mountain. The three, not climbers and without climbing equipment, were attacked by a swarm of bees at about 3:45 on a beautiful autumn afternoon. One of the men attempted to outrun the stinging bees but fell off the cliff, plunging 150 feet to his death. The other two men hunkered down in a rock hollow, pursued by thousands of angry bees. The mountain was closed down, and dozens of firefighters, including some in white bee suits, swarmed over the cliff to rescue the men, who were each stung over 300 times. The bees also descended down to the Echo Canyon parking lot where they stung several hikers.

Another disturbing killer bee incident occurred on the first weekend of May 2013 when 55-year-old Steven Johnson, a rock climber from Tucson, Arizona, with thirty years of experience, was attacked by a swarm of bees while bolting a route on a remote cliff in the Santa Rita Mountains. Johnson was found on Monday, May 6, hanging from his harness on a rope 70 feet above the ground. Both he and his dog, which was found on the top of the cliff, were dead from bee stings. It appeared that Johnson was drilling holes and pounding bolts into them for a new route. His hammering apparently disturbed the bees. He was anchored directly to the wall, so it appeared that the bee swarm was sudden and he was unable to retreat down the route.

Africanized honeybees, a hybrid species of docile European honeybees and a more violent southern African strain, are extremely dangerous. The bees arrived in the United States in 1957 after a beekeeper accidently released twenty-six Tanzanian queen bees and drones that were being used for research. Those bees bred with Brazilian bees, producing the Africanized honeybees, also nicknamed killer bees. The bees reached Arizona in 1993.

The aggressive bees attack if provoked, follow people for over a mile, and sting a lot. It takes at least 500 stings to kill an adult male, although people have received over 1,500 stings and survived. The rule of thumb is that ten stings per pound of body weight equals a fatality, so a 150-pound person would have to be stung 1,500 times to die. The bees are most active on warm days and build hives in protected places like holes and under overhangs.

Experts say to sneak slowly past beehives; don't flail your arms or swat at the bees because they're attracted to movement and any bees you kill secrete isopentyl acetate, a bee pheromone that inflames the other bees and causes them to attack. A single bee sting injects almost 0.1 mg of venom. Bees generally don't go out cruising for trouble, but instead sting in self-defense when they perceive a threat to their hive. The Africanized bees sting in large numbers when they detect a threat within 50 feet of the hive.

The best way to avoid getting swarmed by Africanized honeybees is to simply avoid climbing routes with beehives. This is sometimes more difficult than it sounds, but before climbing a route in Arizona, which is the worst place in the United States for bee attacks, listen for the sounds of bees. There is often a loud humming coming from the hive. Scan the cliff from the ground and find where the hive is located, then decide whether it is too close to your proposed climbing route. If it is too close, either find another route or go to another cliff. Camelback Mountain in Phoenix has a sign at the trailhead warning about possible bee activity. Read it and pay attention. Also remember that bees are less active in the colder winter months.

If you are attacked by bees while climbing, there are few good options. It is best to get down as quickly as possible, which can be difficult if you are leading a pitch and don't have a good lowering anchor available. Descend by rappelling, lowering, or downclimbing. Stay tied into the rope—don't panic and untie and try to escape by free soloing, because you will still get stung and probably take the fatal express route down the cliff. Remember that a fall will almost always be fatal, whereas you can survive hundreds of bee stings.

Climb with Zero Impact

Phoenix and the surrounding mountain ranges lie in the Sonoran Desert ecosystem, an area characterized by extreme temperatures and giant cacti. Desert ecosystems and environments are extremely fragile and sensitive to human use. The human marks linger for a long time on this arid landscape. Irrigation canals built by the ancient Hohokam Indians over a thousand years ago can still be seen. More recent scars include old mines, social trails, and damage from off-road vehicles and motorcycles.

Every desert climber should adopt a zero-impact ethic to minimize his or her impact on this beautiful land. The trails in the Phoenix area are heavily used and sometimes abused. As trail users and climbers, we need to pay attention to the impact that our hiking and climbing has on the landscape. If we all obey some commonsense rules for desert hiking, we can ensure that these fabulous areas will remain as a wild enclave from the encroaching city.

Climb, as always, at your own risk and take responsibility for your actions. Demonstrate to other users, including hikers and mountain bikers, that climbers are a responsible user group.

To minimize your impact, follow these three Falcon zero-impact principles:

- Leave with everything you brought.
- Leave no sign of your visit.
- Leave the landscape as you found it.

Always stay on the trail. Cutting switchbacks or traveling cross-country causes erosion and destroys plants. Often a trail is braided; try to follow the main route whenever possible. The desert is very susceptible to erosion caused by unthinking off-trail hiking. Follow existing climber's trails to the cliffs. These paths are sometimes hard to follow, so take your time initially to find the right trail.

Pack it in—pack it out. Everything you carry and use, including food wrappers, orange peels, cigarette butts, and plastic bottles, needs to come out with you. Carry a plastic bag for picking up other trash along the trail.

Respect public and private property, livestock fences, and mining claims. Federal laws protect all archaeological and historic antiquities, including Indian ruins and artifacts, petroglyphs, fossilized bone and wood, and historic sites. Don't pick flowers, pick up rocks, or take anything with you when you leave. If everyone took just one item, it wouldn't be long before nothing was left. Enjoy their beauty, but leave all natural features for other climbers and hikers to enjoy.

Properly dispose of human waste by digging a hole 4 to 6 inches deep and at least 300 feet from water sources and dry washes. Do not burn or bury toilet paper. Instead, pack it out in a plastic baggie. The best thing to do, of course, is to use the public restrooms that are found at the trailheads described in this book.

Pete Takeda surveys a steep headwall on Hard Drivin' on Tom's Thumb.

The Kachinas: Arizona's First Climbing Club

While climbers probably scrambled on Camelback Mountain's cliffs and Phoenix outcrops before World War II, they left no records of their ascents. After the war a troop of Boy Scouts organized the Kachina Mountain Club, the first known climbers in the Valley of the Sun. The Kachinas pioneered rock climbing in the Valley, learning rope skills, belaying, rappelling, pitoncraft, and climbing safety.

The Kachinas began in the mid-1940s when Ray Garner, a flight instructor for the US Army, dropped by a meeting of Boy Scout Troop 9 one night and enthralled them with mountaineering tales. Bob Owens, a retired judge in St. George, Utah, and one of the original Kachinas, recalls, "There would not have been a Kachina Mountain Club without him. He learned to climb on the Palisades of the Hudson River and then was a guide in the Tetons. Ray had a charismatic personality, lots of ideas, kept the guys spellbound at Kachina meetings, and was a gutsy and good climber."

An article by Joseph Stocker in the December 1949 issue of *Boy's Life* recalled that first meeting: "He [Garner] described something of the mountaineer's technique and told them about the implements that a climber uses. He tried to convey . . . the magic of climbing, its excitement and challenge, the profound satisfaction that comes when you reach the summit."

Ben Pedrick and Ed George were the first scouts to go rock climbing with Garner, doing practice routes around Phoenix and then climbing the Four Peaks in the Mazatzal Range. In 1947 the group established a senior scout group focused on climbing. They named themselves, said Bob Owens, the Kachinas, "since the Hopi Kachinas live in mountains and must have been rock climbers like us." The outfit included Ben Pedrick and his brother Lee, Ed George, Jim Colburn, Dick Hart, Dick McMorris, Bob Owens, and Win Akin, who died at age 20 in a fall on Nez Perce in the Tetons in 1948.

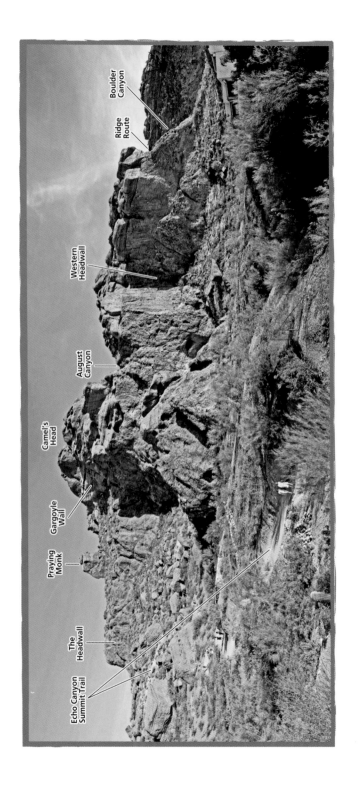

available along the street before the lot. Parking is a problem on busy days, especially weekends and mornings. Consider carpooling with friends to the trailhead. Park only in designated areas along the entrance road and at the trailhead lot. Police will ticket parking offenders. The recreation area and trails are open from sunrise to sunset. Dogs are prohibited on all trails in the Echo Canyon area. For more information contact Echo Canyon Recreation Area, 5700 N. Echo Canyon Pkwy.; (602) 261-8318.

Access to the climbing sectors is from the Echo Canyon Trailhead (GPS: 33.521328 N / -111.973433 W). To reach The Headwall, Praying Monk, and Gargoyle Wall, hike 0.4 mile up the 1.3-mile-long Echo Canyon Summit Trail to a saddle north of the cliffs. At a large trailside boulder (GPS: 33.520757 N / -111.972157 W), a 0.3-mile climber trail climbs the hill to the southwest to the left side of The Headwall and the left side of the Class 3 Gully (GPS: 33.520450 N / -111.970139 W), the easiest access route to the Praying Monk and Gargoyle Wall.

To reach the Western Headwall, including the Suicide area, hike up the summit trail for 0.2 mile and go right on a trail toward a ramada. Keep left and descend to a wash, then follow a trail southwest for 0.1 mile to a large boulder on the right. Scramble up a short climber's trail to the base of Suicide. To start Ridge Route, continue on the trail from the boulder another 0.1 mile, then scramble up to the base of the route. To find 3-Star Nightmare, follow the trail from the boulder for 0.2 mile until the big face is directly south. Scramble up to the route base.

Climbers enjoy the evening on the summit of the Praying Monk

THE HEADWALL

The Headwall is a northwest-facing cliff band that lies south of a large boulder where the summit trail reaches a saddle. Hike up a climber's path to the base of the cliff. Four easy routes on the left side of the wall allow access to the upper terrace routes, including the routes on Praying Monk. Most of the routes are loose, so use caution pulling out on handholds. Also check the bolts and anchor bolts on the routes, as they do occasionally loosen in the Camelback choss rock. Wear a helmet when climbing and belaying on these routes.

Descent: Descend from the upper terrace by downclimbing Class 3 Gully or, preferably, by making a single-rope rappel from a large eyebolt atop Rappel Gully. The bolt is hard to find initially because it hides below a large boulder above the gully and can't be seen from above. It's wise to clip into the bolt while setting up the rappel rope.

Hike along the cliff base from Class 3 Gully to access the other routes. Routes are listed left to right.

1. Class 3 Gully (3rd class) Easy but risky. Rope up if you're unsure of your abilities. Climb an easy gully or ridge on the left side of the wall. Cross behind a small, detached pillar and scramble up another gully to the upper terrace.

2. The Walk-Up (4th class) Not exactly walking. Climb easy rock up a gully 70 feet right of Class 3 Gully and scramble to the upper terrace.

3. Rappel Gully (5.4 R) Climb a recessed gully with hard-to-find pro to a ledge with an eyebolt below a

large boulder. This is the best rappel route from the upper terrace.

4. Headwall Route (5.4) Good pitch to access the upper terrace. Climb a shallow water groove past four bolts to a 2-bolt anchor. Scramble up a gully onto the terrace.

5. Rain of Terror (5.8) Climb a well-protected black streak and groove. 9 bolts to 2-bolt anchor. 90 feet.

6. Sleazy Street (5.6) Right of Rain of Terror on the left side of a buttress. Good climbing on chunky rock. 9 bolts to 2-bolt anchor. 90 feet.

7. Donamatrix (5.8+) 2 pitches. Climbs an obvious groove with a dark streak on the right side. **Pitch 1:** Climb the bolted groove and water stain to a 2-bolt anchor in a scoop. **Pitch 2:** Continue up the bolted groove to a 2-bolt anchor on the left. 16 bolts. 200 feet.

    Descent: Rappel the route.

8. Ghastly Rubberfat (5.10b) Climb steep bolted rock to easier moves up high and anchors. Stay on the line for the better rock. 7 bolts to 2-bolt anchor.

9. Cameltoe (5.11b/c) Steep and technical bolted route with a crux dyno on the right side of The Headwall. 5 bolts to 2-bolt anchor. 55 feet.

10. Spicebox (5.10b) 3 pitches. Good climbing and good rock on the far right side of the wall. Begin on white rock right of a gully. **Pitch 1:** Climb chunky rock (5.6) to a ledge. 2 bolts to 2-bolt anchor. **Pitch 2:** Climb a well-protected face (5.10b) to a high anchor. 12 bolts to 2-bolt anchor. **Pitch 3:** Climb another short easy pitch to anchors. 2 bolts to 2-bolt anchor. Many parties end atop pitch 2.

    Descent: Rappel the route. Best to use a 230-foot (70-meter rope), but a 200-foot (60-meter) just works. Tie stopper knots in the rope ends. **FA:** Mark Trainor and Manny Rangel.

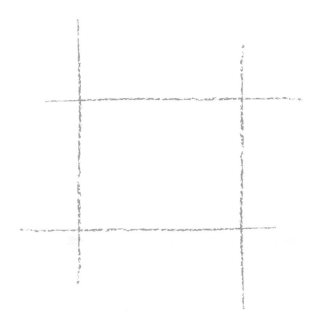

PRAYING MONK

The Praying Monk, an 80-foot-high tower perched on the east side of the upper terrace, is a Phoenix landmark that looks like a kneeling monk. The best route on the tower is the East Face with the Southeast Corner start. The rounded summit offers a great view that includes Squaw Peak, the McDowell Mountains, Pinnacle Peak, Four Peaks, and the western escarpment of the Superstition Mountains. Praying Monk summit GPS: 33.519649 N / -111.969559 W.

1. East Face (5.6) No topo. A Phoenix classic first climbed on December 26, 1951, by former city mayor Gary Driggs and Guy Mehl. Traditionally rated 5.2. Start at the southeast corner below a large boulder leaning against the corner. Climb up left into a shallow cave formed by the boulder and the main face. Traverse up right around a corner to the left side of the east face and follow five bolts to the summit anchor bolt. 120 feet.

Descent: Make a single-rope, mostly free rappel from rap bolts on the south side of the summit. **Rack:** Quickdraws and a 200-foot (60-meter) rope.

2. Southeast Corner (5.6) No topo. A direct start to route 1, East Face that makes it a better route. Begin below the southeast corner of the tower. Face climb up right (5.6) to the first bolt, pull onto a stance above to the second bolt, step right around the corner onto the east face, and climb cobbles to the summit anchors—a rappel eyebolt and two belay bolts. 7 bolts. 120 feet.

Descent: Make a single-rope, mostly free rappel from the large eyebolt on the south side of the summit. **Rack:** Quickdraws and a 200-foot (60-meter) rope.

GARGOYLE WALL

This high north-facing cliff, with some of Camelback's best routes, is southwest of the Praying Monk. Most of the routes are clean and free of loose rock. Be cautious of bees on the wall, especially on the upper Hart Route. Do not climb any routes that exhibit bee activity, and retreat if any bees are present.

Access the cliff by climbing one of The Headwall routes and following a climber's path on the upper terrace to the cliff base. Routes are listed left to right.

1. Dr. Demento (5.11d) Start uphill from the Praying Monk on the left side of the wall.

2. Pedrick's Chimney (5.1) An obvious chimney on the left side of the cliff. Scramble to the highest point of the talus field. Climb an easy open dihedral to the base of the chimney. Climb the chimney past a few bolts to a large eyebolt and belay. The summit of the Camel's Head is easily reached from here by scrambling right along a ledge system to the Hart Route. Climb the Friction Slab pitch to an anchor. Scramble up left from here up gullies to the Camel's Head summit.

Descent: Rappel 90 feet from the eyebolt. This is the standard descent for many of the routes that reach the summit of the Camel's Head.

Pedrick's Chimney, one of the earliest technical routes on Camelback Mountain, was first climbed by Ben Pedrick in 1946, accompanied by a boy named Curtis. Bob Owens, one of the early Kachinas, said, "He climbed it both up and down without aid, and there was no sign of a previous climb. He said prayers first." In 1946 and 1947, two other notable routes were climbed—Hart Route by Dick Hart and George Route by Ed George.

3. Misgivings (5.9 R) 4 pitches. Ascends a blank wall 140 feet right of Pedrick's Chimney. **Pitch 1:** Work up right along a thin crack on an easy ramp to a bolt. Climb up left past old bolts and surmount a steeper headwall (5.9) to a 2-bolt belay on a ledge. **Pitch 2:** Traverse left about 25 feet and then climb to a belay ledge. **Pitch 3:** Climb up right to a large ledge that runs across the face. **Pitch 4:** Traverse left across the ledge and then downclimb to the top of Pedrick's Chimney.

Descent: Rappel 90 feet from the eyebolt anchor.

4. Hart Route (5.3) 4 pitches. An easy classic climb. Start on the left side of a large buttress in the middle of the face. **Pitch 1:** Climb an easy gully up right past a bolt to a 2-bolt anchor on a ledge. **Pitch 2:** Continue up the gully/groove, passing an overhang on the left, to a chimney and a good belay ledge. An alternate variation start climbs a deep chimney and gully (5.2) to the base of the Friction Pitch. **Pitch 3:** The Friction Pitch. Move the belay by scrambling up right in a short gully to the base of a slab. Friction and smear for 60 feet up the slab to a 2-bolt anchor. **Pitch 4:** Climb an easy face past a couple of bolts to the top. Continue up left up gullies to the top of the Camel's Head.

Descent: From the Head summit, scramble back to the anchor atop pitch 3. Rappel down to the ledge and scramble east along the ledge system to the top of Pedrick's Chimney. Rappel 90 feet from the eyebolt anchor. **Rack:** Wired nuts and cams.

5. Chimera (5.9) 2 pitches. Good climbing on good rock. Begin just right of a deep gully (alternate start to Hart Route). **Pitch 1:** Face climb along a black streak to a belay anchor on a small ledge. 9 bolts to 2-bolt anchor. 110 feet. **Pitch 2:** Climb steep rock (5.9) left of a black streak to a pothole. Continue up easier rock to anchors on a ledge. 10 bolts to 2-bolt anchor. 130 feet.

Descent: Scramble to the Hart Route anchors to the left. Rappel or downclimb to a large ledge and scramble east along it (4th class) to

Jim Waugh belays
Martha Morris on 3-Star
Nightmare, a long
face climbing pitch on
Camelback Mountain.

the eyebolt anchor above Pedrick's Chimney. Rappel 90 feet to the cliff base.

6. Hard Times (5.7+) 3 pitches. Begin west of a deep gully below two large holes. Start below the right-hand hole. **Pitch 1:** Climb easy rock for 25 feet to the right hole. Duck through an archway into the left hole and belay from a bolt. **Pitch 2:** Climb up the rib between the two holes to a bolt. Continue up the face above (5.7) past three more bolts to a belay stance atop a boulder inclusion. 7 bolts to 2-bolt anchor. Most parties rap here. **Pitch 3:** The route continues another pitch by working straight up past a bolt to a ramp system that leads up right to ledges.

Descent: Make a two-rope rappel from the 2-bolt anchor atop pitch 2. **Rack:** Cams to 2 inches for first pitch and quickdraws.

7. Aerial Combat (5.9+ R) 3 pitches. Good face climbing on the wall's right side. Begin left of double potholes and a long crack system (Beehive Route). **Pitch 1:** Climb up right past a crux at bolt 2, then up left to anchors at a stance. 8 bolts to 2-bolt anchor. 120 feet. **Pitch 2:** Climb up right past three bolts. Continue up left past newer bolts to anchors on a ledge. 9 bolts to 2-bolt anchor. 125 feet. **Pitch**

3: Traverse right on a ledge system to a bolt, then climb a black streak to a large ledge at the top of the wall. Go right into a gully and belay from a tree.

Descent: Scramble across ledges above the route to the top of Pedrick's Chimney. Downclimb Pedrick's Friction Pitch and cross ledges to an eyebolt anchor above the chimney. Rappel 90 feet to the upper terrace.

8. Unknown (5.10a) 3 pitches. Start below a vertical crack system (Beehive Route). **Pitch 1:** Climb the crack system, then up right to a crux (5.10a) at bolt 3. Continue following bolts (5.9) to the left side of a ledge. Go right to an anchor. 10 bolts to 2-bolt anchor. 100 feet. **Pitch 2:** Go back left on the belay ledge. Climb directly up steep rock with several bulge cruxes to a belay ledge up right. Scramble 15 feet right to the hidden ledge. 12 bolts to 2-bolt anchor. 100 feet. **Pitch 3:** Climb easier bolted rock past a short crux (5.8) to a 2-bolt anchor.

Descent: Scramble east across the top of the wall to the top of Pedrick's Chimney. Downclimb the Friction Pitch and scramble across a ledge system to an eyebolt rappel anchor above the chimney. Rappel 90 feet. **Rack:** Fourteen quickdraws plus slings for bolt anchors.

The following route is right of Boulder Canyon, the deep canyon around the buttress right (west) of Suicide.

5. 3-Star Nightmare (5.8) A long, loose pitch that's not for 5.8 leaders. Look for a line of bolts up the left side of a large, steep face left of the Camel's Ear in the southwest corner of the park. Scramble up left to a belay bolt on a ramp. Climb the left side of a black water streak up the face to a small cave with a belay and rappel anchor. 11 bolts to 4-bolt anchor.

Descent: Make a double-rope, 150-foot rappel to the cliff base.

Pinnacle Peak

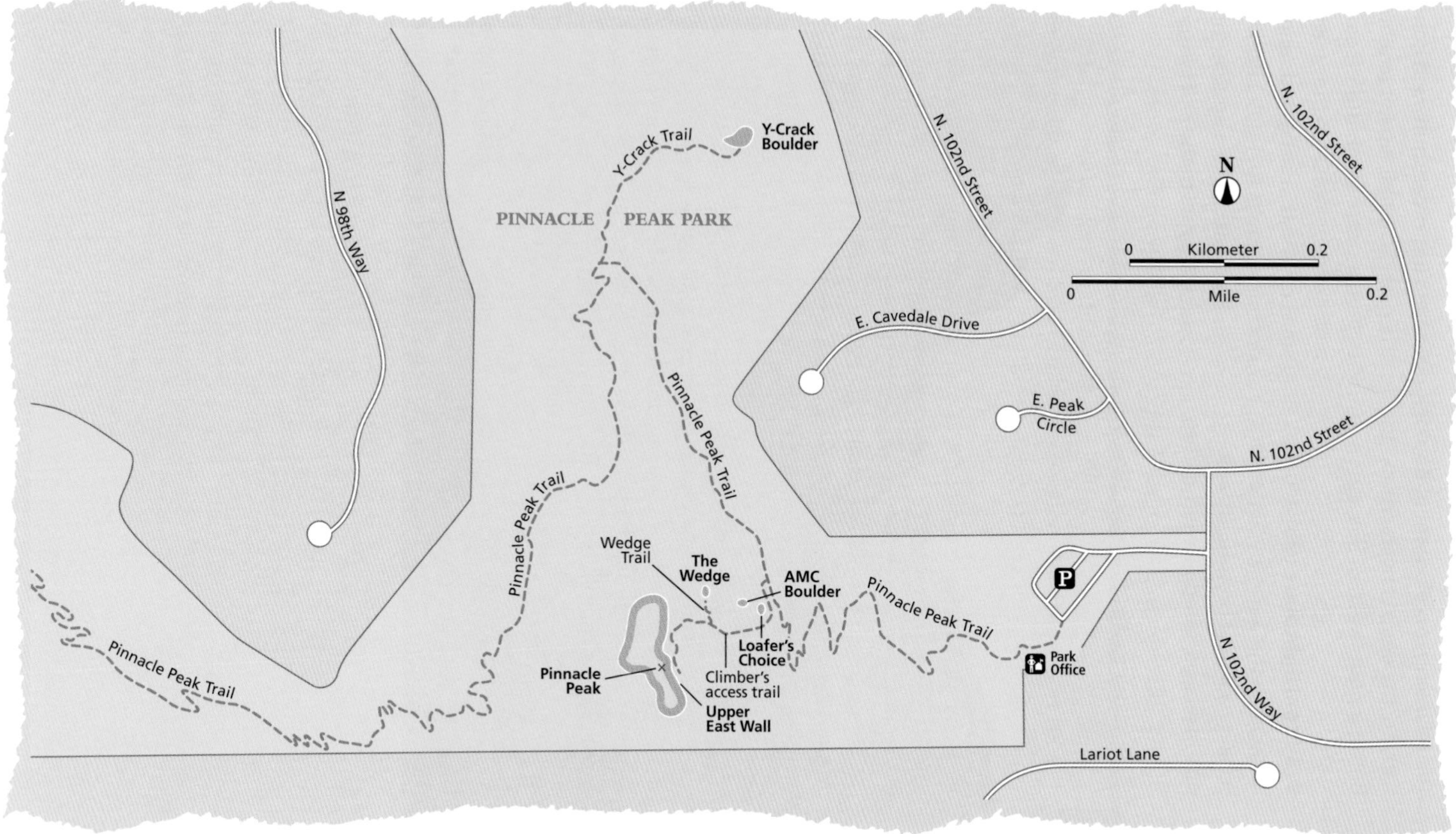

N. 102nd Street

N. 102nd Street

N. 102nd Street

N 102nd Way

N

0 0.2 0.2
Kilometer

0 0.2
Mile

E. Peak Circle

E. Cavedale Drive

Lariot Lane

P

Park Office

Pinnacle Peak Trail

Y-Crack Boulder

Y-Crack Trail

PINNACLE PEAK PARK

Pinnacle Peak Trail

AMC Boulder

Loafer's Choice

Climber's access trail

The Wedge

Wedge Trail

Upper East Wall

Pinnacle Peak

Pinnacle Peak Trail

N 98th Way

Pinnacle Peak Trail

Pinnacle Peak

Pinnacle Peak, a prominent 3,169-foot granite tower on the northeast edge of Scottsdale, rises above a sprawl of subdivisions. The peak, along with smaller satellite crags, boasts an excellent selection of quality crack climbs and bolted face routes. The area, easily accessible from Phoenix and its suburbs, has more five-star climbs than any other local crag, making it a worthy destination and the best climbing area near Phoenix.

Access, however, was a big problem at Pinnacle Peak in the 1990s. The surrounding area was annexed by Scottsdale in 1982 and then protected as a 185-acre park in 1985. In 1994, 35 acres were sold to a developer in exchange for building a visitor center and trail. During this period, Pinnacle Peak was closed to recreational use, including climbing and hiking. The park reopened in 2002 as a 150-acre city parkland.

Brian Shelton jams Short but Sweet's awkward crack on the Y-Crack Boulder at Pinnacle Peak.

Rock climbing is allowed in three areas of the park, and includes a wide variety of routes and grades. Pinnacle Peak Park is open during daylight hours; check the park website (www .scottsdaleaz.gov/parks/pinnacle -peak-park) for summer and winter hours. Park users must leave by dusk. Follow the climber's access trails up the slopes below the east face and from the ridge north of the peak. Watch for rattlesnakes during the warmer months and bring plenty of water. No dogs are allowed in the park.

Getting there: The easiest access is via Scottsdale Road or Pima Road from AZ 101, which loops north from US 60 and east from I-17. Drive north on either Scottsdale or Pima, then turn east onto Happy Valley Road and drive to Alma School Road. Make a left (north) onto Alma School Road. Follow Alma School until it bends right and make a designated left turn onto North 102nd Way to Pinnacle Peak Park. A ninety-space parking lot, small visitor center, and trailhead (GPS: 33.727855 N / -111.860311 W) are located on the west side of the road. Water is available at the trailhead. Additional parking is on North 102nd Way. Contact Pinnacle Peak Park, 26802 N. 102nd Way, Scottsdale, AZ 85262; (480) 312-0990.

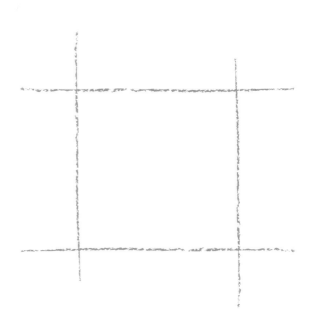

AMC BOULDER

This large, east-facing boulder, named for the Arizona Mountaineering Club, sits halfway up the hillside below Pinnacle Peak. The routes are good leads and topropes. Descend off the summit by rappelling east from an eyebolt. Routes are listed left to right.

1. Reunion (5.8 R) Route on the left side of the face; often toproped. Thin face moves protected by two bolts lead up the face left of the Varicose crack. Place gear in the crack to remove the R rating.

2. Varicose (5.6) Fun climbing. Climb the left-hand crack on the face with jams and laybacks. The crack starts wide, then pinches down. Bring a #5 Camalot to protect the bottom, or run it out to a higher placement. **Rack:** Camalots #5, #4, and #3 to medium sizes.

3. Rurpture (5.10b) Thin face moves lead past a bolt to a right-angling crack. Above, edge past a couple more leaning cracks to bolt anchors at the top. **Rack:** Small to medium nuts and cams to 1 inch.

4. Mickey Mantle (5.8) Climb a slab with a bolt, then up right along a crack to a blunt arête. Step off a flake, mantle past a bulge and bolt, then cruise to summit anchors. **Rack:** Nuts and small to medium cams.

LOAFER'S CHOICE SLAB

This popular east-facing slab is just north of the AMC Boulder. Access it by hiking up Pinnacle Peak Trail to the marked climber's access trail on the left. Follow it up the slope to Loafer's Choice. Bolt anchors, backed up with cams, for belaying and toproping are on the top.

5. Loafer's Choice (5.10a R) Good sustained face climbing. Climb a short, left-facing corner to a steep slab left of an arête. Work up the tricky slab with continuous moves. Belay in a hole, or climb the runout face to the right to a 2-bolt anchor on top. 4 bolts.

   Descent: Walk off.

6. Dead Meat (5.7) Right of Loafer's Choice. Edge up a face protected by a bolt to a small roof at a horizontal crack. Pull over the roof with crystals, then climb the slab above left of a short crack to a bolt by an arête. Follow the arête to a stance, clip a bolt, and finish up a pebbled face.

   Descent: Walk off. **Rack:** Couple of medium cams.

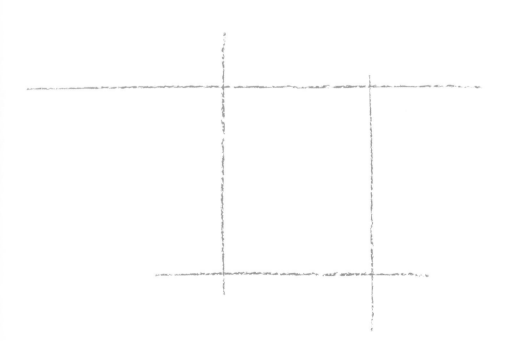

THE WEDGE

The Wedge, a wedge-shaped, 45-foot-high block, sits higher on the slope above the AMC Boulder. The boulder offers several fun routes.

Descent: Descend with a single-rope rappel from a 2-bolt summit anchor.

7. Naked Edge (5.9) Cool route on the right side of the southeast face. Watch your rope on the arête. Begin left of the east arête. Work up a thin finger crack and corner and finish up the arête. 3 bolts to 2-bolt anchor.

8. Redemption (5.9) Classic hard route put up by Dane and Lance Daugherty in 1968. Up the left side of the southeast face. Start near the middle of the face and climb up left to a high first bolt. Thin face moves right of the arête lead to another bolt. Grab the arête above and carefully climb to the top. 2 bolts to 2-bolt summit anchor. A variation start begins on the left side of the arête. Climb past a glue-in bolt and muscle around the arête to the face.

9. Hiliter (5.7 R) No topo. Another Daugherty route that is the only bolted line on the northwest face. Thin face moves lead to a high bolt. Continue smearing up crystals past another bolt to a 2-bolt anchor on the summit. 45 feet.

Beardsley Boulder Pile

Beardsley Boulder Pile is a group of granite boulders on the east flank of a low 2,075-foot mountain between Beardsley Road and Deer Valley Road in north Phoenix. This is a fun and easily accessible area for a quick outing. Over 100 boulder problems that range in difficulty from V0 to V7 scatter along the northeast base of the mountain. On the hillside above the boulders are several small crags with both bolted and traditional routes. Get beta on the boulder problems and routes in *Beardsley Boulder Pile*, a fold-out topo guide by Marty Karabin.

Getting there: The area is in north Phoenix, about 5 miles east of I-17. The easiest approach is from AZ 101. Take exit 28 onto Cave Creek Road and drive north 0.5 mile to East Lone Cactus Drive. Turn left and drive west on Lone Cactus for 0.4 mile until it dead-ends by the mountain and park beside the road (GPS: 33.680442 N / -112.037767 W). Most of the boulders are scattered along the mountain base; the cliffs are on the slopes above.

PINNACLE PEAK EAST FACE

Pinnacle Peak's East Face and Upper East Wall, both facing the parking lot and visitor center, offer great climbing up cracks and steep faces. Routes 1 through 7 are on the Upper East Wall, while the other lines climb the upper bulging face. Routes are described from left to right.

Upper East Wall

The Upper East Wall is a 90-foot-high, east-facing cliff with a variety of crack and face climbs that end on a wide, slabby ridge. The Sun Deck Boulder, a prominent flat-topped boulder, sits atop the ridge directly below Pinnacle Peak's South Face. The East Wall climbs are used as access routes to Sun Deck Boulder and the routes on the South Face. The easiest route to the boulder is the first pitch of South Crack.

Access the wall by following the climber's access trail from the Pinnacle Peak Trail up left around the AMC Boulder, then up slopes and along Pinnacle Peak's base to the wall.

Descent from the routes is by scrambling south along the ridgeline and downclimbing 4th-class rock.

1. Mr. Creamjeans (5.10d) Carefully edge up a steep slab with one bolt on the left side of the face. Belay atop blocks.

2. Birthday Party (5.7) Excellent moderate climbing. Face climb up a right-facing dihedral with two bolts to a right-angling crack. Traverse up right under a long, narrow roof and jam an obvious crack (5.7 hands) over the roof to a belay ledge. **Rack:** Wired nuts and medium to large cams to 3 inches.

3. Pecker Party (5.10b) Begin at Birthday Party. Climb up right along a diagonal crack and ramp, then edge past three bolts (5.10b) to a roof. Traverse right and finish up an easy crack. **Rack:** Several cams.

4. Dried Oatmeal (5.10b R) Start right of Pecker Party below a corner capped by a roof. Climb the easy corner to the roof, traverse left, and face climb up a blunt prow (5.10b) with four bolts to an easy right-leaning crack. **Rack:** Stoppers and a few medium to large cams.

5. Boxer (5.7) Begin at the start of Dried Oatmeal. Work up a right-angling crack to a stance. Climb an easy slab to a face traverse under a roof, jam over the roof (5.7), and finish up a crack to a belay by Sun Deck Boulder. **Rack:** Medium to large cams.

6. Beegee (5.11a) A roof problem that was Phoenix's first 5.11. Climb right up a flared crack (5.10c) to a ledge. An easy slab leads to a short, overhanging roof crack (5.11a). Follow a groove above to a belay at Sun Deck Boulder. **Rack:** Medium nuts and cams.

7. South Crack (5.5) 2 pitches. Classic moderate route to Pinnacle Peak's summit and one of Phoenix's best beginner trad leads. Start below a chimney system on the southeast side of the formation. **Pitch 1:** Easy climbing (4th class) leads up a crack system to the Sun Deck Boulder below the South Face. **Pitch 2:** Climb over a large, triangular-shaped boulder to a wide crack. Continue up a chimney past a bolt to a set of bolt anchors that can be used for an intermediate belay. Continue up the chimney to a ledge, then up a crack to the east summit and three eyebolts.

Descent: Make two single-rope rappels. **Rappel 1:** Rappel 50 feet from three bolts to a notch north of the summit. **Rappel 2:** Rappel from two bolts to the base of the East Face. **Rack:** Medium to large nuts and cams.

East Face

The East Face of Pinnacle Peak is a steep, smooth wall of granite that's home to some of Phoenix's best face climbing routes. The routes were established in the late 1970s and early 1980s by a hardcore crew of local climbers, including Stan Mish, Dave Black, Jim Waugh, Glen Rink, and Pete Noebels.

Descent off the top of the routes is the same as South Crack—two single-rope rappels. **Rappel 1:** Rappel 50 feet from three bolts to a notch north of the summit. **Rappel 2:** Rappel from two bolts to the base of the East Face.

8. Hades (5.10b) Start right of South Crack. Climb a short chimney to a 30-foot, right-angling off-width crack. Belay on a ledge. Finish by scrambling up left to South Crack and Sun Deck Boulder, or do one of the East Face routes. **Rack:** #3 to #6 Camalots.

9. Name It (5.6) Easiest access pitch to the base of the upper East Face. Begin right of Hades below a right-angling crack. Jam and face climb up cracks to a belay ledge with a bolt under a roof and the East Face.

Descent: Scramble south on ledges to Sun Deck Boulder. **Rack:** Medium to large cams.

10. Fear of Flying (5.10c) Face climbing classic and one of Pinnacle Peak's best climbs. Start at Hades's belay below the roof. Move up right and then climb left along an angling crack under a small roof (5.10c) to the left edge of the East Face. Face climb up the left side of a blunt arête with three bolts and past a horizontal crack with a fixed pin (5.10b). Continue to the summit with more thin moves (5.10b).

Descent: Make two single-rope rappels. **Rack:** Stoppers, TCUs, and cams to 2 inches.

11. Powder Puff Direct (5.11a) Airy, exposed, and excellent. Begin right of Name It from that route's belay. Work up a short, right-facing corner right of a roof and step left onto the steep face. Hard face climbing leads straight up past five bolts to the summit.

Descent: Make two single-rope rappels. **Rack:** Stoppers and small cams.

12. Lesson in Discipline (5.11c) Hard, desperate face climbing on perfect granite—an intimidating Phoenix classic. Start at Hades's belay. Climb a short corner, then downclimb right to a thin crack. Work up the crack (5.11a) to a bolt and then face climb steep rock past more bolts. Above, the angle and difficulty eases. Pass the fourth bolt and follow a crack and face to the summit.

Descent: Make two single-rope rappels. **Rack:** Stoppers and small cams.

13. Sidewinder (5.11c) Another face climbing masterpiece. First free ascent was a 1979 flash by Peter Noebels. Begin right of Powder Puff Direct.

Traverse right along a horizontal crack that arcs around the right corner of the face. Work up the strenuous crack (5.11a) until you can move right into an off-width crack. Follow to a stance and continue up a face (5.9) to the top.

Descent: Make two single-rope rappels. **Rack:** Stoppers and small to large cams.

South Face

The steep South Face towers above Sun Deck Boulder. Reach the base of the face by climbing one of the East Face routes (10 to 13) or by scrambling up 4th-class rock on the south side of the formation. Routes are listed right to left.

Descent: From the top, make two single-rope rappels from the east summit. **Rappel 1:** Rappel 50 feet from three bolts to a notch north of the summit. **Rappel 2:** Rappel from two bolts to the base of the East Face. If you finish on the west summit, make a jump across to the east summit and bolt anchors.

14. Shalayly Direct (5.11c) 3-star classic. Sustained and excellent. Begin on Sun Deck Boulder. Face climb up right past four bolts (5.11a) and then traverse right to a flake crack (5.9). Follow the crack (5.9) and face climb up thin edges (5.11c) past three more bolts to the summit. 8 bolts.

Descent: Make two single-rope rappels. **Rack:** Stoppers, TCUs, and small to medium cams.

15. Silhouette (5.8) Begin at Sun Deck Boulder. Climb the first 50 feet of South Crack into a chimney. Stem and step left on a steep slab, then face climb past three bolts up a rock rib to a horizontal crack. Move up right to the fourth bolt and edge (5.8) to the top. 4 bolts.

Descent: Make two single-rope rappels. **Rack:** Medium and large cams.

16. Twenty-Eighth Day (5.9 R) 1 or 2 pitches. Recommended. Begin at Sun Deck Boulder. **Pitch 1:** Climb the first few feet of South Crack to a glue-in bolt and a ledge out left. Face climb up left to an inverted flake. Climb past the right side of the flake to a small ledge, step left along the ledge, and move up the face and corner above past a bolt to a belay ledge. An alternative is to place a medium cam in the horizontal crack and climb for the top. **Pitch 2:** Climb the short face above (5.9) past two bolts to the summit.

Descent: Make two single-rope rappels. **Rack:** Wired nuts and small to medium cams. Use slings on gear to avoid rope drag, especially if you do it in one pitch.

17. Never Never Land (5.11a) Excellent route with sustained, exposed face climbing. Start left of Sun Deck Boulder below South Gully, a gully-chimney. Climb the gully until you can traverse left along a horizontal crack (5.7) to a small ledge.

Climbers finish up Short but Sweet's final face in fading light.

Thin face climbing (5.11a) heads up the face above past four bolts to the west summit. 4 bolts.

Descent: Jump to the east summit and make two single-rope rappels. **Rack:** Wired nuts and small to medium cams.

18. South of Heaven (5.11c) Begin off a pointed boulder left of South Gully. Thin face moves lead past two bolts to a horizontal crack. Edge and smear the steep face above past eight more bolts to the summit. 10 bolts.

Descent: Jump to the east summit and make two single-rope rappels.

Y-CRACK BOULDER

The Y-Crack Boulder, actually a small formation, not a boulder, is named for a prominent Y-shaped crack system on its south face. The formation is on a rounded ridge north of Pinnacle Peak, and is easily accessed by a climber's trail from the northernmost point of the Pinnacle Peak Trail.

Descent is by rappelling off the 2-bolt anchor on the north side of the summit.

1. Y-Crack (5.9+) Brutal, strenuous, leaning off-width crack on the south face. Thrutch up the crack, using laybacks on a flake to a tough off-width section. Finish with more laybacks. Keep left at the Y junction to a 2-bolt summit anchor. **Rack:** Off-width gear—a couple #6 and #5 Camalots or Big Bros. Most climbers toprope it. Climb Turtle Piss on the back side to access the anchors.

2. Short but Sweet (5.8+) Another Pinnacle Peak sandbag. Awkward, tricky start to good hand jams in double left-leaning cracks. Finish up the face above a ledge to the summit anchors. **Rack:** Medium to large cams.

3. Turtle Piss (5.6) No topo. Face climb up the northeast side of the block past two bolts to a 2-bolt summit anchor.

Pete Takeda edges up Hard Drivin' on the east face of Tom's Thumb.

McDowell Mountains

The McDowell Mountains, towering over 2,000 feet above the surrounding valleys, form a ragged skyline of 3,000- and 4,000-foot-high peaks across northeastern Phoenix. The northwest-trending range, pinched by encroaching suburban growth, offers, along with neighboring Pinnacle Peak, Phoenix's best climbing opportunities.

The McDowell Mountains, named for General Irwin McDowell, were long a desolate and arid wilderness, inhabited first by the Hohokam and later the Yavapai Indians. Prospectors found little gold here, preferring to concentrate their efforts on the richer promises held by the Superstition and Bradshaw Mountains. For years, cowboys frequented the rocky McDowell slopes, where each head of cattle required 350 acres a year of desert scrub.

The McDowell Mountains, preserved by the McDowell Sonoran Preserve and McDowell Mountain Regional Park, offer lots of great climbing on granite cliffs on the north slopes of the range. These popular crags include Sven Slab, Gardener's Wall, the striking 160-foot-high monolith of Tom's Thumb, and the Girlie Man area. The cliffs are composed of an abrasive, compact granite that has weathered into steep slabs studded with edges, knobs, and thin flakes and steep walls split by vertical crack systems. For more information on over 240 routes and more cliffs, consult the comprehensive guidebook *McDowell Rock: A Climber's Guide* (2016) by Erik Filsinger and Cheryl Beaver.

The cliffs in the McDowell Mountains, easily accessed from Scottsdale and AZ 101, are in

The 1970s were the golden age of McDowell climbing. Most of the classic testpiece cracks were jammed, including Deep Freeze on Tom's Thumb. Jim Waugh, who did the first free ascent with Stan Mish in 1978, called it "One of the best climbs in Phoenix!" In his Phoenix rock climbing guidebook, Waugh recalls the 1978 first ascent of Ubangy Lips on the Thumb. "On the first ascent bolt hangers were forgotten. The leader had to tie-off the bolt driver to finish the lead. Gulp!!!!!!"

McDowell Sonoran Preserve, a natural area with more than 30,000 acres administered by the City of Scottsdale. Climbers need to obey the preserve rules for continued access to this historic climbing area. These rules include:

- Follow designated climber's access trails to all cliffs.
- Climbing is allowed only on designated cliffs.
- Climb only during posted hours of operation.
- Obey any closures of cliffs or areas.
- No new fixed anchors may be installed.
- Unroped climbing is not recommended.
- Dogs must be leashed and dog waste picked up and disposed of properly.
- Tom's Thumb may be seasonally closed for raptor nesting; obey all wildlife closures.

Follow a Leave No Trace ethic when climbing and hiking here. Carry plenty of water, particularly in hot weather, and wear a hat. Keep an eye out for rattlesnakes among the boulders and bushes during the warmer months. Watch for beehives on the cliffs.

Bring a standard rack for trad routes, including one to two sets of Friends, a set of TCUs, a set of wired nuts, and quickdraws. Sets of RPs and a large Camalot are useful on some routes. Bring two 165-foot (50-meter) ropes for climbing and rappelling, although many routes can be safely climbed with a 200-foot (60-meter) rope.

Getting there: The easiest way to reach the Tom's Thumb Trailhead from Phoenix and Scottsdale is to drive on the AZ 101/Pima Freeway and exit onto either Scottsdale Road or Pima Road. Drive north on North Scottsdale Road or North Pima Road to Happy Valley Road and turn right (east). Drive east on Happy Valley Road, passing the junction with North Alma School Road, which leads to Pinnacle Peak just to the north. Continue east on East Happy Valley Road around the south side of Troon Mountain, following signs for Tom's Thumb Trailhead. East Happy Valley Road slowly bends north, passing through suburbs, and where it becomes North 118th Street, turn right (east) on Ranch Gate Road. Follow Ranch Gate Road east to North 128th Street. Turn right (south) on North 128th Street and follow the narrow paved road south to two parking loops and the Tom's Thumb Trailhead. The trailhead (GPS: 33.694109 N / -111.801942 W) is on the south end of the east parking lot near a big steel shelter with restrooms (no water). The street address is 23015 N. 128th St., Scottsdale, AZ 85255.

McDowell Mountains North

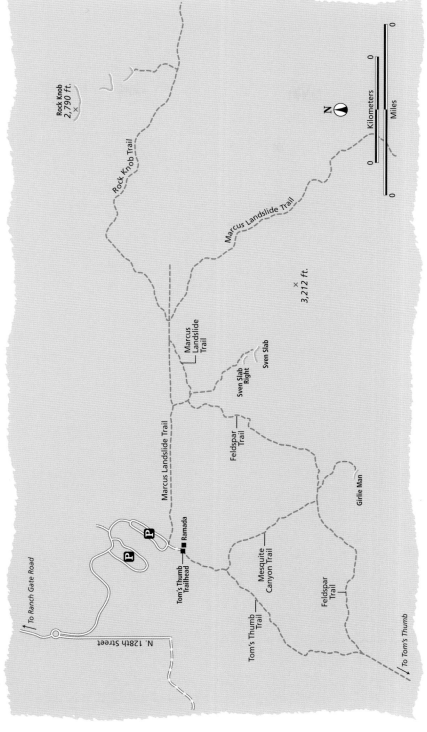

To Ranch Gate Road

N. 128th Street

P

P

Tom's Thumb
Trailhead

Ramada

Marcus Landslide Trail

Rock Knob Trail

Rock Knob
2,790 ft.

Marcus
Landslide
Trail

Marcus Landslide Trail

Sven Slab
Right

Sven Slab

Feldspar
Trail

3,212 ft.

Girlie Man

Mesquite
Canyon Trail

Feldspar
Trail

Tom's Thumb
Trail

To Tom's Thumb

N

Kilometers

Miles

0

0

0

0

0

McDowell Mountains

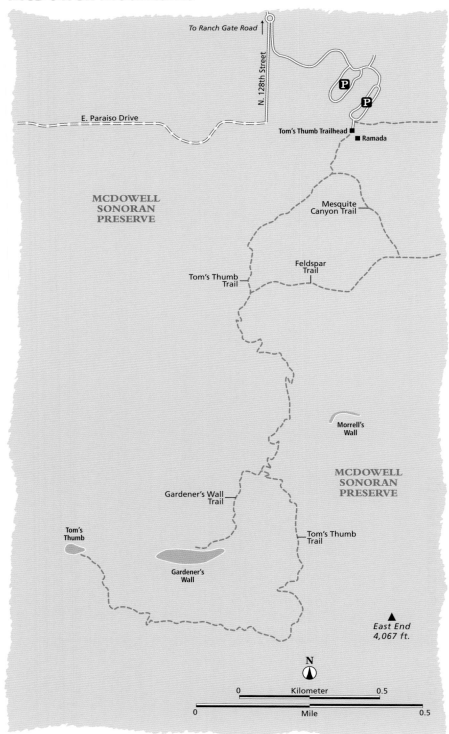

To Ranch Gate Road ↑

N. 128th Street

P

P

E. Paraiso Drive

Tom's Thumb Trailhead ■
■ Ramada

MCDOWELL
SONORAN
PRESERVE

Mesquite
Canyon Trail

Feldspar
Trail

Tom's Thumb
Trail

Morrell's
Wall

MCDOWELL
SONORAN
PRESERVE

Gardener's Wall
Trail

Tom's
Thumb

Tom's Thumb
Trail

Gardener's
Wall

▲
East End
4,067 ft.

N

| 0 | Kilometer | 0.5 |

| 0 | Mile | 0.5 |

Two trails to the different climbing sectors begin at the trailhead. The Tom's Thumb Trail goes south to access Gardener's Wall and Tom's Thumb. The Marcus Landslide Trail goes east to access Girlie Man, Sven Slab, and Rock Knob. Consult each cliff description for directions.

GIRLIE MAN

The Girlie Man sector is a fun climbing area with bolted slabs and a few cracks. The easy and moderate routes are popular with beginners, groups, and guide services. Girlie Man is a good toproping site, because it is easy to set up topropes from bolt anchors above each route. The east-facing cliff, broken by ledges, boulders, and bushes, is reached by a short hike from Tom's Thumb Trailhead on the north side of the McDowells.

The area is a compact sector with three slabs that face east on the west side of a broad canyon floored by a sandy wash. All the routes are worth climbing but are runout at easier sections. Descent off all routes is by lowering from bolt anchors or rappelling. The rappel off Sassy requires a doubled 70-meter rope, two ropes, or two rappels with a single rope. Routes are described from left to right when facing the cliff.

Getting there: From the eastern parking area and large ramada, hike east on Marcus Landslide Trail for 0.2 mile to its junction with Feldspar Trail. Go right (south) on Feldspar Trail for 0.4 mile to a marked climber's access trail to Girlie Man, Sven Tower, and Hog Heaven climbing sectors near a large boulder. Go left (south) on the climber's trail and hike up a dry wash, then scramble up a signed climber's

A climber smears up Smoother, a delicate slab route at the Girlie Man area.

trail that leads to the base of the Girlie Man slab. Hiking distance is 0.6 mile.

Alternatively, hike south from the ramada on Tom's Thumb Trail for 0.1 mile to a junction with Mesquite Canyon Trail. Go left (east) on Mesquite Canyon Trail for 0.2 mile to Feldspar Trail. Go left on Feldspar Trail for 0.1 mile to the climber's access trail to Girlie Man, just north of the huge boulder. Go right (south) on the climber's access trail and hike up a dry wash, then scramble up a signed climber's trail that leads to the Girlie Man slab. Hiking distance is 0.5 mile.

1. Girl's Best Friend (5.3 R) Good beginner route on the far left side of the main slab. Friction up the slab to

bolt anchors on a ledge. 3 bolts to 2-bolt anchor. 50 feet.

2. Smoother (5.8 R) Fun but tricky route, especially for novices, but with a short crux section. Delicate slab climbing with thin edges and smears leads to the third bolt. Climb easier rock to anchors on a ledge. 3 bolts to 2-bolt anchor. 60 feet.

3. Dog Gone It (5.7 R) Another fun outing at a moderate grade. Start right of Smoother and left of a rounded indentation. Climb a short, steep face up right to a sloping jug below a horizontal crack. Continue past the crack on low-angle terrain, then finish up left to a narrow shelf

and Smoother's anchors. 4 bolts to 2-bolt anchor. 60 feet.

4. Sassy (5.2 R) Great beginner climb and a good route to learn basic trad climbing skills. Start below an obvious right-facing dihedral with a tree halfway up. Layback, jam, and smear up the low-angle dihedral to the tree. Belay here or traverse right to a 2-bolt anchor for a two-pitch climb. Continue up the easy dihedral to a 2-bolt anchor on the slab up left at the top. 110 feet.
   Descent: Rappel the route with a doubled 70-meter rope or make two rappels from bolt anchors. **Rack:** Double set of cams from 0.5 inch to 4 inches; medium and large Stoppers are useful.

5. Pastie Whitie (5.6 R) Good slab climbing. Smear up a trough to a bolt, then continue up a clean white slab past a second bolt and run it out to anchors at a stance. Belay here or continue up the Sassy dihedral to the summit anchors. 2 bolts to 2-bolt

anchor. 70 feet. If you climb Sassy's pitch 2, clip the anchors then motor up the right-facing dihedral past another bolt to a 2-bolt anchor. 115 feet.
   Descent: Make a doubled 70-meter rappel from the top anchors or two rappels down the route.

The next two routes are on a clean northeast-facing shield of granite. Access the routes from the base of Pastie Whitie by scrambling up boulders on the right.

6. Girlie Man (5.9+ R) Thin and delicate face climbing. Edge and smear up the left side of the steep slab to anchors. 3 bolts to 2-bolt anchor. 65 feet.

7. Sphincter Boy (5.9 R) Start below a prominent thin crack. Jam the right-leaning finger crack, then finish up the steep clean face above to Girlie Man's anchors. 65 feet. **Rack:** TCUs and cams.

A climber smears up Sven Slab, a popular granite cliff on the northeast side of the McDowell Mountains. LOGAN BERNDT

Sven Slab

Sven Slab Right

SVEN SLAB

Sven Slab is an excellent, north-facing cliff that offers a selection of accessible and mostly bolted routes. The crag, named for a Sven saw used by the first climbing party to hack a trail through dense vegetation to the cliff's base, is a 10-minute hike from the parking area. It's popular on weekends and with guided parties.

Getting there: Park at Tom's Thumb Trailhead on the north side of the McDowells. From the south end of the east parking area, hike east on Marcus Landslide Trail for 0.3 mile.

Just past the right turn to Feldspar Trail, turn right on the marked Sven Slab climber's trail. Follow the trail for 0.1 mile south up a wash, then up brushy slopes past the lower area to the base of the slab (GPS: 33.692495, N / -111.795487 W). Hiking time is 15 minutes. Routes are listed right to left.

1. Hippity Hop (5.6 R) Begin on the far right side of the face in a crevice between boulders and a huge flake. Stem up an obvious flared slot/crack to a boulder-filled chimney. Traverse left onto the face of a pillar and climb

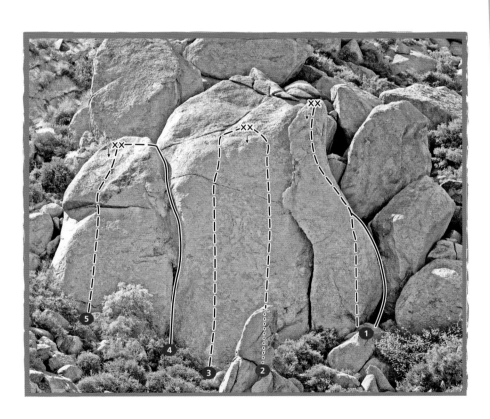

past a bolt to a 2-bolt anchor at the top. A variation start begins off boulders on the left face of the flake. Climb crystals for 15 feet to a bolt. Continue up right on thin face moves (5.10d R) and follow an easier ridge to anchors.

Descent: Rappel or lower from anchors.

2. Nit Nat (5.10a) Begin left of a prominent squeeze chimney. Climb 10 feet to a flake, then pull over the flake and climb 25 feet to a bolt. Climb up left 15 feet to the second bolt and then edge up a steeper headwall past another bolt to a runout slab finish. 3 bolts.

Descent: Walk off. **Rack:** Small and medium cams.

3. Changes in Latitude (5.10b) Begin on the left side of the main block. Climb a delicate, runout slab for 25 feet to the first bolt. Continue past another bolt to a thin headwall to a runout slab.

Descent: Walk off.

4. Peaches and Cream (5.7) The obvious crack between big blocks. Climb a fist crack to a large chockstone in a chimney (sling for pro). Stem past an overhanging, off-width section and thrutch up an off-width to the top.

Descent: Walk off left.

5. Dark Passage (5.10c) Bolted route on the left block. Thin face climbing past three bolts to a horizontal break. Watch for a possible beehive! Pull over a break and cruise an easy slab.

Descent: Walk off left.

6. Quaker Oats (5.5) Fun route and fine beginner lead. The right bolt line on the right side of Sven Slab. Begin on the right side of the white slab. Scramble right onto boulders and belay. Climb up left on a ramp to the first bolt. Continue straight up on excellent rock with great holds to an eyebolt belay on a ledge with trees. 5 bolts.

Descent: Rappel 110 feet with two ropes or single 70-meter rope. A 200-foot (60-meter) rope reaches the ledge to the right with rope stretch.

7. Colorado Crosscut (5.6) Fun left-traversing route. Begin at the Quaker Oats belay boulders (cams in crack for anchor). Traverse up left on the ramp to the first bolt on Quaker Oats. Continue up left past the second bolt on Sinkso, then left to a large flake (gear) and the third bolt on Cakewalk. Work up left on thin edges to another bolt. Move left to edge moves (5.6) that lead to a wide, right-angling crack (#3 Camalot). Climb the crack up right to the eyebolt belay. 4 bolts.

Descent: Rappel 110 feet with two ropes or single 70-meter rope.

8. Sinkso (5.8 R) Tricky below and above the first bolt. Begin at the cliff base left of a large boulder. Delicately climb (5.8) 15 feet to the first bolt. Continue up left (5.8) above the bolt, with groundfall potential below the second bolt. Angle right to the third bolt and motor up an easier slab to the eyebolt belay. 3 bolts.

Descent: Rappel 110 feet with two ropes or single 70-meter rope.

9. Ego Trip (5.7 R) Old, black hangers on bolts and a little runout. Begin on a boulder near a small tree. Climb 15 feet (5.7) to the first bolt. Continue up right another 15 feet to the second bolt (possible groundfall), then grab good edges to an inverted flake (small Friend). Face climb straight up on good edges past another bolt to the eyebolt belay. 3 bolts.

Descent: Rappel 110 feet with two ropes or single 70-meter rope.

10. Cakewalk (5.8) Begin off a large boulder 15 feet left of Ego Trip. Face climb on good edges (5.7) to the first bolt. Entertaining and continuous moves for the next 15 feet lead to bolt 2 at a horizontal break. Climb up right on good edges to the third bolt, then up easier rock past another bolt to the eyebolt ledge belay. 4 bolts.

Descent: Rappel 110 feet with two ropes or single 70-meter rope.

11. Black Death (5.8) Begin by a triangular flake left of Cakewalk.

Climb 10 feet to the top of the flake. Put pro in a right-leaning crack and make delicate face moves up left to the first bolt. Climb a left-facing, layback flake to bolt 2 and then climb easier rock to a right-angling crack that leads to the eyebolt belay. 2 bolts.

Descent: Rappel 110 feet with two ropes or single 70-meter rope.
Rack: Medium Stoppers and small to medium cams.

More routes are found on the upper left side of Sven Slab. These include the excellent crack route One for the Road (5.6). Consult the guidebook *McDowell Rock: A Climber's Guide* (2016) for information on these and other nearby routes.

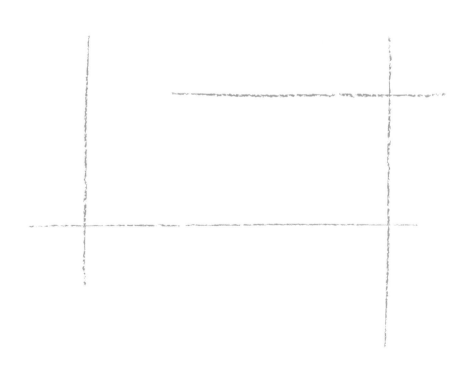

ROCK KNOB

The Rock Knob climbing sector, also called Knob Hill, is a long, low ridge dotted with small cliffs and a jumble of boulders that lies northeast of Sven Slab and stands apart from the main McDowell Mountains massif. Numerous trad and bolted routes scatter across the area, but most are short. This is a fun off-the-beaten-track area to explore with a rope and a rack. The described routes are on southeast-facing Last Light Slab, the Knob's tallest cliff.

Getting there: Begin from the south end of the east loop of the parking area at Tom's Thumb Trailhead (GPS: 33.681824 N / -111.807403 W).

Hike east on Marcus Landslide Trail for 0.5 mile, passing the Sven Slab turnoff, to a junction with Rock Knob Trail (GPS: 33.694503 N / -111.794161 WS). Go left on Rock Knob Trail and hike another 0.6 mile until you're in a wide wash south of the slab. At 0.5 mile the trail leads into the McDowell Sonoran Preserve and passes through a fence into McDowell Mountain Park (GPS: 33.695010 N / -111.787401 W). From the wash, hike north on an unmarked climber's trail for 0.1 mile to the cliff base (GPS: 33.695842 N / -111.786536 W). Allow 25 minutes to hike the 1.2 miles from car to cliff on gentle terrain. Routes are described from left to right.

Brian Shelton climbs Last Light up a steep slab on Rock Knob on the northern edge of the McDowell Mountains.

1. Last Light (5.7) Good clean climbing up the left side of the slab. Edge and smear directly up the slab to anchors. 4 bolts to 2-bolt anchor.

2. Blue Light (5.3 R) Easy beginner route. Climb the low-angle slab on the right up flakes. At the top, either traverse left to Last Light's anchor or continue up to a gear anchor at boulders.

GARDENER'S WALL

Gardener's Wall is an excellent, northeast-facing cliff that offers a selection of mostly moderate face and crack routes on a wide, slabby wall. Most of the routes are worthwhile outings on compact granite with adequate protection. The 300-foot-high cliff is sometimes too cold in winter for comfortable climbing, but it offers shade and indirect sun in spring and fall.

Descent off the wall is by rappelling from three sets of bolt anchors scattered across the summit ridge. Rappel The Phantom with double ropes to the ground. Rappel Renaissance Direct with two 70-meter ropes to the ground. Rappel down Hanging Gardens with two double-rope rappels. You can also scramble off the back side of the wall and follow trails around the east side and back to the cliff base.

Getting there: Park at Tom's Thumb Trailhead on the north side of the McDowells. From the south end of the east parking area, start at the big ramada and hike south on Tom's Thumb Trail for 0.5 mile to the junction with Feldspar Trail on the left. Continue south on Tom's Thumb Trail and ascend steep slopes. At 1.1 miles look for a Rock Climbing Access Route sign on the right marked Gardener's Wall. Go right on this narrow path and hike 0.3 mile southwest across a rocky ravine to the base of Gardener's Wall (GPS: 33.681824 N / -111.807403 W). Routes are described from left to right.

1. Southeast Arête (5.10b) No topo. A short route up the slabby left faces of two large blocks on the far left side of the wall. Climb to a bolt, continue up easier rock, and finish up a blunt arête with two bolts.

Descent: Scramble off left.

2. The Phantom (5.7) 2 pitches. Begin off large boulders below the left side of the wall and left of a deep chimney. **Pitch 1:** Climb a finger crack (5.7) that trends up left to a good belay ledge. **Pitch 2:** Move up left along a low-angle crack above a bush. Follow flakes and cracks up left, then up the airy ridge to a 2-bolt skyline belay stance.

Descent: Rappel 135 feet from anchors to the ground with two ropes, or traverse the summit ridge and do two double-rope rappels down Hanging Gardens.

3. Gobs of Knobs (5.8) 5 short pitches for anyone who's climbed everything else here. This girdle traverse of the face from left to right yields "gobs of knobs" for your hands. Variations are possible. Begin on boulders at the start of The Phantom. **Pitch 1:** Jam The Phantom's first-pitch crack (5.7) to a good belay ledge. **Pitch 2:** Climb easy cracks up left to a right-angling crack. Traverse up right to crack's end. Edge over to another thin, horizontal crack (5.8). Belay in the wide crack (Kreuser's Chimney). **Pitch 3:** Traverse right to Renaissance Direct's third bolt. Continue right across a brushy gully crack to a slab (Fearless Leader's fifth bolt) and downclimb right across a slab to Hanging Garden's 2-bolt belay. **Pitch 4:** Traverse right (5.6) past two bolts to a tree-covered ledge. Belay above the ledge. **Pitch 5:** Swing over the left side of a roof and slab climb (5.6) to the cliff summit.

Descent: Make two double-rope rappels down Hanging Gardens in the wall's center. **Rack:** Selection of wired nuts, small to medium cams, and quickdraws.

4. Kreuser's Chimney Direct (5.3) 2 pitches. Begin below the obvious chimney. **Pitch 1:** Thrutch up the wide chimney to a hole. Squeeze through to a belay ledge on the right with a 2-bolt anchor. **Pitch 2:** Step left into the chimney. Follow the squeeze chimney, then an off-width crack to the summit ridge.

Descent: Make a double-rope rappel from The Phantom's 2-bolt anchor, or two double-rope rappels down Hanging Gardens. **Rack:** Medium to large wired nuts, and cams to 3 inches.

5. Phantom of the Opera (5.10a R) 2 pitches. The R rating comes from a 5.7 runout on pitch 2. Begin right of the chimney, between a boulder and the main wall. **Pitch 1:** Engaging face moves lead up a thin crack (5.10a) to a bush. Move out left and step across the chimney to a horizontal crack. Traverse left a few feet and climb a thin finger crack for 20 feet to a belay ledge. **Pitch 2:** Edge directly up the slab past two bolts to a slashing crack. Run it out above (5.7 R) to the summit ridge and a bolted belay anchor.

Descent: Double-rope rappel from The Phantom's 2-bolt anchor, or two double-rope rappels down Hanging Gardens.

6. Renaissance Direct (5.7) 2 pitches. Superb and well-protected face climbing make this a must-do route for the moderate leader. Local guidebook author Marty Karabin calls it the "best route in the McDowells!" Begin behind boulders. **Pitch 1:** Crisp face moves (5.7) past two bolts lead to a small stance below a thin, right-facing corner. Jam the corner (5.6) to a roof, then pull over and continue up diagonal cracks to a spacious belay ledge with a 2-bolt anchor. **Pitch 2:** Great climbing with fun moves! Climb straight up past four bolts to a summit belay.

Descent: Make two double-rope rappels from a 2-bolt anchor at the top. **Rack:** Small to medium nuts and cams.

7. Fearless Leader (5.10a R) 2 pitches. Start below a steep slab beneath the left side of a hanging flake. **Pitch 1:** Thin face climbing (5.10a) leads past two bolts, then up left to a flake and the third bolt (kind of runout). Continue up to the crack intersection on Hanging Gardens, but then climb straight up the slab above past two more bolts to a 2-bolt belay stance. 130 feet. **Pitch 2:** Move up the slab (5.6) past another bolt to a summit belay.

Descent: Make two double-rope rappels down Hanging Gardens.

8. Hanging Gardens (5.6) 2 pitches. Arizona's best 5.6 route? You decide! Classic moderate route with plentiful

pro, fun moves, and enough exposure to stay interesting. Begin below a large, right-leaning flake in the middle of the wall. **Pitch 1:** Scramble up an easy, left-angling ramp/crack to the base of the flake. Insert pro and climb diagonally up left with hands in a crack to a small stance. Continue up right in a right-angling crack to a 2-bolt belay/rappel station. 100 feet. **Pitch 2:** Diagonal up right in a crack to a bolt and a steeper hand crack that leads to a hanging tree. Keep left via easy cracks and face to a cliff-top belay from gear. 130 feet.

Descent: Scramble east to rappel anchors. Make two double-rope rappels from bolted rappel anchors down the route, or hike off the back side. **Rack:** Small to large cams.

9. Bruisin' and Cruisin' (5.8) 2 pitches. It's "bruisin'" to off-width up the flake or "cruisin'" if you layback it. Easy to toprope from anchors at the end of Hanging Garden's first pitch. Same start as Hanging Gardens. **Pitch 1:** Climb off-width or layback up an obvious right-leaning flake. Pro's harder to get if you layback. At the flake top, traverse up left to Hanging Gardens and finish 20 feet higher at a bolted belay. **Pitch 2:** Not on topo. Face climb directly above the belay past a bolt to a summit belay. 110 feet.

Descent: Make two double-rope rappels down Hanging Gardens from bolted rappel anchors. **Rack:** Medium to large cams.

10. Lickety Split (5.7 R) 2 pitches. Bold slab climbing. Start 25 feet right of Bruisin' and Cruisin' below a narrow, right-leaning arch or atop a flake just right. **Pitch 1:** Layback the arch or stand atop the pointed flake, then move up left and stand on a left-angling crack. Clip a bolt and traverse left along the crack above an overlap. Face climb straight up (hard to get pro—mostly psychological!) for 25 feet to a bolted belay in a shallow scoop. **Pitch 2:** Edge up to a bolt, then angle up right to a bolt at the base of an obvious water groove. Climb the groove (5.7 R, no pro) to a bushy crack. Keep left of the trees and finish up top.

Descent: Make two double-rope rappels down Hanging Gardens from bolted belay anchors. **Rack:** Wired nuts, TCUs, and small to medium cams.

11. For Crying Out Loud (5.10d) 2 pitches. Hard and serious. Same start as Lickety Split. **Pitch 1:** Stand on the pointed flake, step up left into the horizontal crack, clip the bolt, and edge up 15 feet to another bolt. Angle right to a small stance and bolt. Move along the right edge of the slab above a steep wall for 15 feet to the fourth bolt. Traverse up right to a vegetated crack, then follow the angling crack to another bolt. Climb up and right below a large block to a gully and belay. Avoid belaying on the tree-covered ledge because it's an owl nesting site. 5 bolts. **Pitch 2:** Climb up left below a roof. Step over the roof on its left edge and face climb up a slab to the summit. 3 bolts.

Descent: Scramble east along the summit ridge to rappel anchors. Make two double-rope rappels down Hanging Gardens from bolted anchors. **Rack:** RPs, wired nuts, and small to medium cams.

TOM'S THUMB

Tom's Thumb is an obvious blocky, thumb-shaped tower perched high atop a ridge in the northern McDowell Mountains. The 3,970-foot Thumb, named for local 1960s climber Tom Kreuser, offers a great selection of classic crack and face routes, as well as marvelous views of the surrounding valleys, ranges, and subdivisions.

While many hikers reach the base of Tom's Thumb now on a new trail, you will probably see few climbers up there. For a great full-day moderate climbing adventure, climb one of the routes on Gardener's Wall like Renaissance Direct or Hanging Gardens, then scramble down the wall's back side, hike over to Tom's Thumb, and climb Treiber's Deception.

The hike to the Thumb is 4.6 miles round-trip, with 1,420 feet of round-trip elevation gain (1,025 feet net elevation gain), and requires an hour of steady uphill hiking to approach the formation. No water is found at the trailhead or along the way, so pack plenty of liquids to stay hydrated on hot days.

Descent: The standard descent route off the top of Tom's Thumb is to make a two-rope, 140-foot rappel off bolt anchors on the west side of the summit.

Getting there: Access the formation from the parking lot and Tom's Thumb Trailhead on the north side of McDowell Sonoran Preserve. Begin

Tom's Thumb was originally called The Dork by Dick Hart and Bill McMorris after its first ascent in 1948. That name, however, fell into obscurity. Tom Kreuser, Diana Hartrum, and Bill Sewery climbed the landmark peak on September 19, 1964, and reported their ascent to the Arizona Mountaineering Club. Because Kreuser was the first club member to climb the formation, club president Doug Black dubbed it Tom's Thumb. Later the City of Scottsdale asked the US Board of Geographic Names to officially call it Tom's Thumb, but the request was turned down because no names are allowed that honor living people.

Climbers on Hard Drivin', a great two-pitch climb up the east face of Tom's Thumb.

at the south end of the east parking lot at the trailhead (GPS: 33.681824 N / -111.807403 W). Hike south on Tom's Thumb Trail to a junction with Feldspar Trail at 0.5 mile at the mountain base. Continue hiking up the good trail, reaching the junction with the Gardener's Wall climber's access trail at 1.1 miles. Stay left; the trail continues climbing, then levels out at the junction with East End Trail at 1.6 miles (GPS: 33.679157 N / -111.803985 W). Keep right on the main trail and hike past Glass Dome to the junction with Lookout Trail at 2.1 miles. Keep right on Tom's Thumb Trail and follow the trail through boulders to the base of the East Face at 2.3 miles (GPS: 33.681656 N / -111.811223 W).

Routes are described counterclockwise on the freestanding formation, starting with Treiber's Deception at the southeast corner.

East Face

1. Treiber's Deception (5.7) Superb climbing on a classic line. Begin on the left (south) side of the East Face beside a boulder and below an obvious crack system. Chimney up between the boulder and the main wall until it's possible to pull into a flake crack about 15 feet off the ground. Follow the broken crack above to a small ledge with a large block. Climb easy cracks up left onto the skyline. Clip a bolt and edge up the face above to the base of an off-width crack. Work up the crack, using face holds inside, past another bolt to another wide crack. Crank it to the summit. 140 feet.

Descent: Traverse west across the summit to a 3-bolt anchor. Rappel 140 feet with double ropes to the ground. **Rack:** Wired nuts and cams to 4 inches.

2. Hot Line (5.10b) Sustained and exposed pitch. The left crack of an obvious left-angling crack system. Start 25 feet right of Treiber's Deception on boulders below the crack. Jam the awkward, left-hand finger crack (5.9) to a small alcove. Continue up left along the crack to the left side of a wedged block. Jam a steep, flared crack past a fingery section to a large flake. An airy traverse right for 10 feet leads to a flared hand and fist crack finish.

Descent: Traverse west across the summit to a 3-bolt anchor. Rappel 140 feet with double ropes to the ground. **Rack:** Medium to large cams.

3. Hard Drivin' (5.10b or 5.11a) 2 pitches. Excellent route established by John Ficker and Jim Waugh in 1981. Begin below a pointed boulder on the outside face of a pillar. **Pitch 1:** Edge up the pointed boulder for 30 feet (5.10a start and no pro) to its top. Reach across the gap and clip a bolt. Face climb (5.10b) up left on the pillar past three more bolts to a 2-bolt belay ledge. Bring a #1.5 Friend or medium

Rappel off west face

70° XX

nut for a hidden crack between the first and second bolts. Rap 70 feet from here or climb **Pitch 2:** Start on the right side of the ledge. Climb over horizontal overlaps to a bolt. Hard face moves (5.11a) lead to a horizontal crack. Follow it up and right onto the summit and a belay bolt.

Descent: Traverse the summit to its west end and rappel 140 feet with two ropes from a 3-bolt anchor. **Rack:** Quickdraws, wired nuts, and small to medium cams.

North Face

4. Ubangy Lips (5.10c) The 1978 first ascent party of Jim Waugh and Dave Black forgot a bolt hanger, so the drill was tied off for pro! Scramble through a tunnel in the boulders right of Hard Drivin' to the base of an obvious crack with a pod. Chimney up between boulders and the cliff until it's possible to climb flakes (5.9) up to the crack. Jam a good crack to a flare and into the "Ubangy Lips" pod. Exit the pod up a thin, discontinuous crack to face holds (5.10c) and a single bolt. Above, face climb up a thin crack to a wide crack finish. 150 feet.

Descent: Traverse the summit to its west end and rappel 140 feet with two ropes from three bolts. **Rack:** Wired nuts and small to medium cams.

5. Pretty Girls Make Graves (5.12a) Brilliant sustained climbing that requires edging technique and mind

control. Don't fall—it's a long way between bolts. Start right of Ubangy Lips at the base of a blunt arête. Face climb up the arête with small flakes and edges past four bolts. Work up left above the fourth bolt to the bolt on Ubangy Lips. Finish up Ubangy Lips to the summit. 150 feet. 6 bolts.

Descent: Rappel 140 feet with double ropes from a 3-bolt anchor on the west side of the summit to the ground. **Rack:** Quickdraws, RPs, wired nuts, TCUs, and a few cams.

6. Sacred Datura Direct (5.9 R) Another good route with superb rock and thin climbing. Begin 10 feet right of Pretty Girls Make Graves below a shallow, left-facing corner. Climb the small corner with a thin crack, then face climb flakes to the right to a bolt (5.9) 30 feet up—pro is hard to find. Step right into a vertical crack system broken by large pockets. Climb the crack past a fixed pin to awkward moves into a scoop alcove. Follow a thinning crack (5.9) above to a hand crack and bolt. Continue up right along thin seams and face climbing (5.8 R) to the summit ridge. 150 feet.

Descent: Rappel 140 feet with double ropes from a 3-bolt anchor on the west side of the summit to the ground. **Rack:** Stoppers and small to medium Friends.

7. Succubus (5.10b) Excellent full-value crack climb. Start right and around a corner 15 feet from Sacred Datura Direct and below a dark,

XX

X
XX   Rappel west
      140'

4th class
to summit

XX
100'

11

4

5

6

7

8   9   10

11   11

Pete Takeda laybacks through the slippery crux of Succubus on the north face of Tom's Thumb.

right-facing box corner. Jam awkward hands up the black corner 20 feet to a V-shaped roof. Thin laybacks and fingerlocks and slick footholds lead up right along the thin crack to a small stance with a bolt. Above, jam a flared fist and off-width crack to the top. 155 feet.

Descent: Rappel 140 feet with double ropes from a 3-bolt anchor on the west side of the summit to the ground. **Rack:** Wired nuts and small to large cams. Big Camalots protect the upper off-width section.

8. Deep Freeze (5.11a) 2 pitches. Jim Waugh, who did the FFA with Stan Mish in 1978, calls this "one of the best climbs in Phoenix!" Start 25 feet right of Succubus beneath an obvious crack system and right of a smooth face. **Pitch 1:** Face climb a thin, discontinuous crack (5.10) or stand atop a boulder and step left into the crack system. Jam a good hand crack up a shallow, left-facing corner. The crack thins to fingers and ascends a difficult bulge. Continue up a narrow, right-facing corner to a bolt. Work past the bolt (5.11a) to discontinuous cracks on yellow-lichened granite with pockets. Belay from two bolts on a ledge up right by a streak of bird shit. **Pitch 2:** Climb past a final bulge (5.11a) onto the final face with two bolts. Move left to the uppermost summit.

Descent: Rappel 140 feet with double ropes from a 3-bolt anchor on the west side of the summit to

the ground. Or rappel 100 feet from the anchors atop pitch 1 to the base. **Rack:** Wired nuts and double set of small to large cams; #4 Camalot may be useful.

9. Pinto Bean (aka Garbanzo Bean Direct) (5.10d) Excellent face climbing on flakes. Start 3 feet right of Deep Freeze. Edge up flakes on a rounded buttress past five bolts to a right-leaning crack. Continue up the wide crack to a bolted belay on blocks. 150 feet.

Descent: Rappel 140 feet west to the ground with double ropes. **Rack:** Quickdraws and medium to large Friends.

10. Garbanzo Bean (5.7) 2 pitches or 1 long pitch. Classic 1973 route with varied climbing. Start 5 feet right of Pinto Bean. **Pitch 1:** Jam a flared hand crack (5.7) to a broken chimney, then climb the broken chimney to a belay stance (watch for bird crap here). **Pitch 2:** At the obvious break, traverse left on the face to Pinto Bean's wide crack. Jam the off-width crack to a bolted belay on boulders atop the Thumb.

Descent: Rappel 140 feet west to the ground with double ropes. **Rack:** Medium to large Friends, with a #4 Camalot.

11. Kreuser's Route (5.4) 2 pitches. A mountaineering adventure, named for Tom Kreuser, that climbs up the northwest corner of the North Face.

Begin up right from Garbanzo Bean on a ledge reached by scrambling. A variation start jams a 5.6 crack right of Garbanzo's start. **Pitch 1:** Work up left on ramps and cracks to a deep chimney. Climb past a fixed piton and belay on a large ledge at a notch. **Pitch 2:** (4th class) Climb up right to an overhang. Skirt it on the right and head to the top.

Descent: Rappel 140 feet with double ropes. **Rack:** Medium to large cams.

West Face

12. The Settlement (5.7) 2 pitches. Good line up the West Face. Begin off a boulder at the base of the face. **Pitch 1:** Climb a large pointed flake, then face climb straight up to a bolt below an overlap. Traverse right below the overlap crack past another bolt to a left-angling corner system. Pull an overhang (5.7) and follow the corner up left to a belay ledge. **Pitch 2:** (4th class) Climb cracks to a blocky ledge. Face climb up right around a roof to the summit.

Descent: Rappel 140 feet with double ropes to the ground. **Rack:** Small to large cams.

13. West Corner (4th class) 2 pitches. The Thumb's classic summit route; first climbed in 1948 by Dick Hart and Bill McMorris. Start 20 feet right of The Settlement at blocks and a tree. **Pitch 1:** Scramble up a ramp (3rd class) to a ledge with trees. **Pitch 2:** Work up wide cracks on the left to a ledge with boulders. Traverse out

Tom's Thumb, perched high on a ridge, offers some of the best climbing around Phoenix.

right below a roof and face climb to the top.

Descent: Rappel 140 feet with double ropes to the ground. **Rack:** Medium to large cams.

14. Face First (5.9+ R) Same start as West Corner, only scramble up the ramp to a belay below a steep slab. Edge up the slab to a thin overlap. Climb above to a bolt to easier climbing that leads to The Settlement's belay. Continue up The Settlement to the top.

Descent: Rappel 140 feet with double ropes to the ground. **Rack:** Small and medium gear.

15. Fatman's Delight (5.6) 2 pitches. **Pitch 1:** Climb West Corner's 3rd-class ramp to a tree, then climb the corner above to a ramp. Climb right and belay at a tree. **Pitch 2:** Work up a short chimney in a left-facing corner to an easy slab finish.

Descent: Rappel 140 feet with double ropes to the ground. **Rack:** Medium to large cams and off-width gear.

South Face

16. Experiment in Terror (5.11c R) 3 pitches. Easy to toprope the first pitch from the ledge above. Rating is height-dependent. Start on the left side of the south face. **Pitch 1:** Face climb up thin, discontinuous seams

to a rusted fixed piton. Jam a fingery crack (5.11c) filled with grass to a belay ledge. 40 feet. **Pitch 2:** Traverse right across a horizontal crack to a short vertical crack on West Face Direct. Climb it to another horizontal crack. Step right and face climb to a ledge. **Pitch 3:** Jam a finger and hand crack (5.8) to the summit bolt anchors.

Descent: Rappel 140 feet with double ropes to the ground. **Rack:** RPs, wired nuts, TCUs, and small to medium cams.

17. Waughbo (5.11a R) Easy to toprope from the ledge above. Begin right of Experiment in Terror below a thin, left-leaning arch. Undercling up the arch, reach up right to a bolt, and step up right onto a narrow ledge. Undercling out a flake crack to a bolt. Face climb flakes to a belay ledge. 50 feet.

Descent: Scramble off left down the West Corner ramp. **Rack:** TCUs and small cams.

18. West Face Direct (5.11d R) 2 pitches. Excellent but stiff edging challenge. Same start as Waughbo. **Pitch 1:** Undercling up the arch, reach up right to a bolt, and step onto a narrow ledge below a flake crack. Undercling right to a bolt and then face climb straight up past two more bolts onto a sloping stance and horizontal crack. Traverse right along horizontal cracks to a vertical crack. Climb that crack to another

horizontal crack. Face climb to the belay ledge on Fatman's Delight. **Pitch 2:** Climb the third pitch of Experiment in Terror.

Descent: Rappel 140 feet with double ropes to the ground. **Rack:** RPs, wired nuts, TCUs, and small to medium cams.

OTHER MCDOWELL CRAGS

The McDowell Mountains are sprinkled with many other good crags with lots of fun routes. Check out *McDowell Rock: A Climber's Guide* (2016) by Erik Filsinger and Cheryl Beaver for the beta on over twenty cliffs and more than 240 routes, many unpublished before. Recommended cliffs include Hog Heaven, Morrell's Wall, Rosetta Stone, and Sven Towers.

Facing page: Pete Takeda jams up Deep Freeze, one of the classic hard routes on Tom's Thumb.

Martha Morris
seconds Sweet
Surprise on
The Loaf.

Little Granite Mountain

Little Granite Mountain, called Granite Mountain on the USGS topographic map, was renamed by climbers in deference to the more famous Granite Mountain outside Prescott. The isolated 3,526-foot-high mountain, protected in the McDowell Sonoran Preserve, rises above a sloped desert plain north of the McDowell Mountains. Numerous small granite crags and boulders scatter across the mountain, offering rock climbers a quiet and remote getaway close to the Phoenix megalopolis. The mountain's pristine Sonoran desert ecosystem, with towering saguaro cacti and other typical desert plants, offers an unusual climbing experience for visiting climbers.

Most of the routes are short, single-pitch lines up bolt-protected faces and slabs, along with occasional crack climbs. Little Granite Mountain offers a wide range of route grades, but is best for easy and moderate climbs. Topropes are easily set up at all the described cliffs, using either gear or bolts for anchors. Good bouldering is found at Morning Glory Boulders on the Bootlegger Trail 0.5 mile from the main parking area.

The mountain's abrasive granite features knobs, dikes, flakes, and edges, as well as more xenoliths, a piece of "foreign rock" trapped in the cooling matrix, than other area granites. Xenoliths, Greek for "strange rocks," are inclusions that are usually black and finer grained than the surrounding granite. They are weather resistant and often form excellent "Thank God"–type holds amid a sea of small granite edges. Xenoliths form when chunks of surrounding rock break off into liquid magma and are not melted.

The best cliffs lie on the southern end of the mountain and are reached by pleasant hiking on good trails through the desert. Climber's trails lead to all the cliffs, but are sometimes hard to initially locate. It's best to pick the easiest route to a crag, and you will eventually run into a trail. Follow existing trails and washes as much as possible to avoid damaging plants and causing erosion. Watch for rattlesnakes on the approach trails and bees on the cliffs.

Getting there: Little Granite Mountain is in north Scottsdale, northeast of Phoenix. All of the cliffs are reached from the Granite Mountain Trailhead at 31402 N. 136th St. To get there, drive north from the Loop 101 freeway on either Scottsdale

Little Granite Mountain

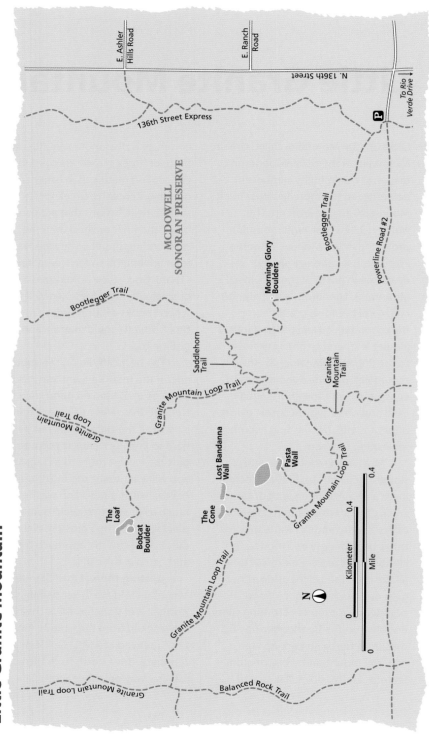

Bobcat Boulder

Bobcat Boulder is the small crag left of the prominent slabby prow on the The Loaf. Some good single-pitch routes ascend the crag's east face. Routes are listed left to right.

Descent: A 2-bolt rappel anchor at the top of Snakes are Poodles Too is easily accessed from any belay station. It's also easy to scramble off the back side and down the gully between Bobcat and The Loaf.

8. Grin and Bear It (5.7) Bobcat's best route. Start at the junction of the south and east faces on the far left side of the cliff. Face climb past two bolts to a roof, pull past on the right to the third bolt, and cruise to the top.

9. Crystalline Grin (5.10c) Thin face moves lead past two bolts on the lower slab to a horizontal crack. Above, move right into a crack system and end on a bushy belay ledge.

10. Snakes are Poodles Too (5.8) Work up an incipient crack system (5.8) to a stance at a horizontal crack. Continue face climbing up cracks to a high bolt, then move up a slab to a break and finish at a 2-bolt anchor below a final headwall, which can be climbed (5.8) to the top.

Granite Mountain rises above Morning Glory Boulders, one of the bouldering areas along the mountain's edge.

11. Missing Lynx (5.8) Begin right of Snakes are Poodles Too. Climb a seam to a crack to a ledge on the far right side of the face. Step left and do fun face moves up the face past two bolts and the right-side arête to the summit.

PASTA WALL

Pasta Wall is a south-facing slab on the far south end of Little Granite Mountain. It offers a fun selection of easy routes, making it great for beginners and novice leaders. Bring a small rack with a few cams and nuts.

Getting there: From the Granite Mountain Trailhead on North 136th Street, hike west on Powerline Road #2 Trail, which follows a closed road below power lines for 0.6 mile. At the first trail junction, go right on Granite Mountain Trail and hike 0.3 mile north to a junction with Granite Mountain Loop Trail. Go left on the loop trail and hike 0.3 mile until directly south of the obvious Pasta Wall. Look for a climber's path that goes right. Follow it north for 0.1 mile to the base of the slab (GPS: 33.773107 N / -111.801060 W), keeping left of a boulder jumble below it. Routes are described from left to right.

Descent: Descent off all routes is by either rappelling or lowering from bolt anchors, or scrambling around the side of the cliff.

1. Half Measures (5.5) Climb the left slab. 2 bolts to 2-bolt anchor.

2. Full Measures (5.6) Up the middle of the left slab. 2 bolts to 2-bolt anchor.

3. Problem Dog (5.3) Climb a right-angling crack up the shield on the left side. Finish up an easy slab to a 2-bolt anchor (same as Half Measures and Full Measures).

4. Negro y Azul (5.6) Left side of the central rock shield. 2 bolts to 2-bolt anchor.

5. Blue Sky (5.7) Smear directly up the central slab past an overlap. 1 bolt to 2-bolt anchor.

6. Crazy Handful of Nothin' (5.5) Climb up a right-angling corner, then up left past the overlap to a 2-bolt anchor.

7. Say My Name (5.6) Climb a short slab, pull over a roof, then climb up right.

LOST BANDANNA WALL

The Lost Bandanna Wall is on the southwest side of Little Granite Mountain. The cliff's ragged top is visible from the parking area to the east. The clean, south-facing cliff offers several good face routes and moderate crack climbs, with good views in a desert environment.

Getting there: From the Granite Mountain Trailhead on North 136th Street, hike west on Powerline Road #2 Trail, following a closed road below power lines, for 0.6 mile. At the first trail junction, go right on Granite Mountain Trail and hike 0.3 mile north to a junction with Granite Mountain Loop Trail. Go left on the loop trail and hike almost half a mile to a bend south of the cliff. Leave the trail here and hike uphill to the base of the cliff (GPS: 33.774682 N / -111.801963 W). Routes are listed left to right.

Descent: The easiest descent is to walk off (either right or left) from the ledge system where the routes end, or rappel from a 2-bolt anchor in the middle of the ledge.

1. Slot (5.6) On the far left side of the wall. Jam the obvious crack up a left-facing dihedral to a good belay ledge. **Rack:** Mostly medium and large cams.

2. Climb at First Sting (5.11b) Start right of Slot. Steep face climbing past three bolts leads to a thin crack. Belay above on a spacious ledge.

3. Limbo (5.6) 2 pitches. Easier than it looks. **Pitch 1:** Work up a right-angling crack system and onto the face above (5.6) to a bolt. Climb up to a belay ledge. Walk off west or climb **Pitch 2:** Climb a short, left-facing corner (5.6) to the summit. **Rack:** Wires and a small selection of cams.

4. Graceland (5.10d) Edge up thin flakes just left of a prow past three bolts to a high, rusty bolt on Limbo. Continue up easier rock to a belay ledge. 4 bolts.

5. Spectrum (5.7) A fun crack. Start below a right-facing corner. Climb a broken crack system up the corner to a 2-bolt anchor on a ledge (same as Lawless and Free). **Rack:** Selection of wired nuts, TCUs, and small to medium cams.

6. Lawless and Free (5.9+) A good face route. Begin left of Loosy Loose. Climb good edges up to the first bolt, pull up right to a bulging protuberance and the second bolt, and continue up a short headwall to easier climbing and the third bolt. Belay from a 2-bolt anchor on a ledge.

7. Loosy Loose (5.11b) Begin just left of two large boulders at the cliff's base. Follow five bolts up the steep, flaky face to a 2-bolt anchor on a ledge.

THE CONE

The Cone, a slabby, south-facing cliff, is west of Lost Bandanna Wall on the southwest slopes of Granite Mountain. The friction routes are sparsely protected. Watch for beehives near the cliff.

Getting there: From the Granite Mountain Trailhead on North 136th Street, hike west on Powerline Road #2 Trail, which follows a closed road below power lines, for 0.6 mile. At the first trail junction, go right on Granite Mountain Trail and hike 0.3 mile north to a junction with Granite Mountain Loop Trail. Go left on the loop trail and hike 0.5 mile until you are directly south of the obvious slab. Scramble through boulders and bushes to the base of the cliff (GPS: 33.774666 N / -111.802660 W). Routes are listed right to left.

Descent: Rappel off a 2-bolt anchor on Kate's Fault, or scramble down the east side of the crag.

1. Three Dopes on a Rope (5.4)
Good beginner route up the crag's
right-hand slab. Edge past bolts to a
thin crack. Follow onto an easy slab
split by a horizontal crack. Belay up
top by a skyline tree. 3 bolts. **Rack:**
Wires and small cams.

2. Sideshow (5.6) Climb the buttress
left of a prominent, bushy crack past
two bolts to a 2-bolt anchor on Kate's
Fault.

3. Kate's Fault (5.9) Work up a slabby
apron in the middle of the left wall to
a bolt below a dark xenolith. Climb
thin face moves on flakes to the
second bolt, then climb to a 2-bolt
anchor.

4. Unknown (5.10-) On the far left
side of the cliff. Climb a slab to a bolt,
then up a groove to the rounded top.

Lookout Mountain

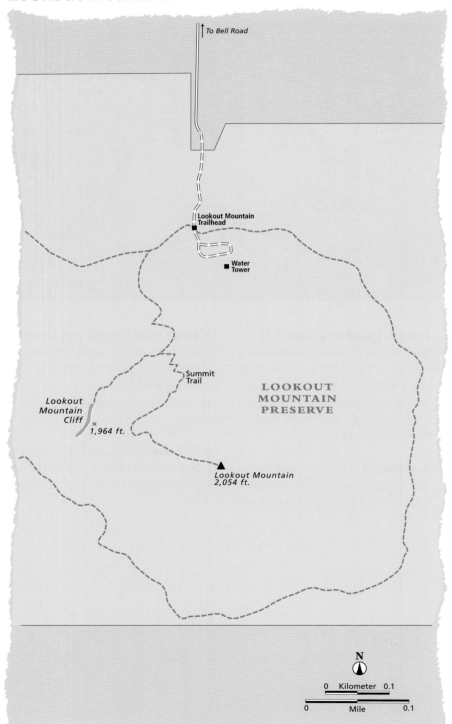

To Bell Road

Lookout Mountain
Trailhead

Water
Tower

Summit
Trail

Lookout
Mountain
Cliff
× 1,964 ft.

LOOKOUT
MOUNTAIN
PRESERVE

▲
Lookout Mountain
2,054 ft.

N

0   Kilometer   0.1

0   Mile   0.1

Lookout Mountain

Lookout Mountain is in the Phoenix Mountain Preserve on the north side of Phoenix. The Dead Dobie Wall, a short, west-facing, basalt cliff, is below the mountain's west summit. The cliff offers a selection of sport routes. Expect good views, privacy, and some loose rock. Most routes have cleaned up since they were bolted in 1993, but wear a helmet anyway when climbing and belaying. It's not the best climbing, but it is accessible sport climbing. Most of the routes were established by Marty Karabin in the 1990s. For more beta on Lookout

Mountain, consult Karabin's fold-out guide *Lookout Mountain Boulder and Climbing Guide.*

Getting there: The Dead Dobie Wall and Lookout Mountain Park are south of Greenway Parkway in north Phoenix. Greenway Parkway intersects I-17 to the west. Cave Creek Road and 32nd Street run north from Phoenix to the parkway. Follow Greenway Parkway to 16th Street and turn south toward the mountain. The road dead-ends at a parking area below the peak (GPS: 33.627164 N / -112.048200 W). Hike southwest

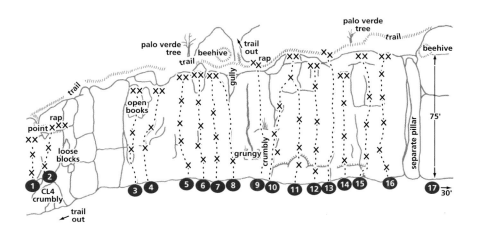

from the lot on Trail 150. When you reach the fourth switchback, go right on the circumference trail for a short distance. Turn left onto a climber's trail that contours up to the cliff on the west side of the west summit (GPS: 33.623822 N / -112.049937 W). Routes are described from left to right.

1. Loose Lieback (5.8) Scramble up a loose 4th-class face to a short 2-bolt face. 2 bolts to 2-bolt anchor.

2. The Gnome (5.10a) Scramble up a loose 4th-class face. Climb a short headwall up right. 2 bolts to 2-bolt anchor.

3. I Love Loosie (5.9 R) Climb an unprotected crack to a 2-bolt face and a corner. 2 bolts to 2-bolt anchor.

4. Junkyard Dog (5.10d) An overhanging crack to a bolted face. 2 bolts to 2-bolt anchor.

5. Speed Freak (5.11b) Recommended. 4 bolts to 2-bolt anchor.

6. When Lester Comes Out to Play (5.11a) 4 bolts to 2-bolt anchor.

7. Little Miss Dangerous (5.10d) Go up right above the third bolt. 3 bolts to 2-bolt anchor.

8. Too Loose to Goose (5.9) Climb past a bolt to a crack. Face climb along a crack to Little Miss Dangerous's anchors. 3 bolts to 2-bolt anchor.

9. Unnamed (5.11a) A toprope right of a grungy crack system. 2-bolt anchor.

10. Falling Stars (5.11d) A loose start to steep rocks. 4 bolts to 2-bolt anchor.

11. The Contender (5.11a) Pull a roof, then face climb good rock. 4 bolts to 2-bolt anchor (same as Falling Stars).

12. Double Feature (5.10c) Double roofs off the ground, then face moves up solid rock. 4 bolts to 2-bolt anchor.

13. Unknown (5.9) The cliff's first route. Tricky moves to a grungy groove and a 2-bolt anchor.

14. Devil in Disguise (5.10b) Strenuous roof start to fun moves up good rock. 3 bolts to 2-bolt anchor.

15. Totally Trad (5.8) Climb out the right side of a low roof, then climb dark rock to anchors. 3 bolts to 2-bolt anchor.

16. Unknown (5.7) One of the best routes on the crag. Left of a broken pillar. 4 bolts to 2-bolt anchor.

17. Pushin' Your Luck (5.9) 30 feet right of the pillar. 3 bolts to 2-bolt anchor.

Superstition Mountains

The Superstition Mountains sprawl across central Arizona east of Phoenix like a rumpled Indian blanket. It's a tangled tapestry of precipitous canyons, sharp volcanic peaks, soaring cliffs, high mesas, and forests of saguaro cacti. Most of this austere and beautiful range is protected in the 160,200-acre Superstition Wilderness Area, the wild centerpiece of 2.9-million-acre Tonto National Forest, one of the nation's largest national forests.

The haunting Superstitions, now nicknamed the Supes, were first called Sierra de la Spuma ("Mountains of Foam") by the Spanish and figure prominently in Arizona mythology as the site of the infamous Lost Dutchman Mine. The search for the mine began in 1892 when a German prospector, Jacob Walz, died of pneumonia in Phoenix. On his deathbed, the old man supposedly revealed a cryptic description of his mine. He said, "There's a great stone face looking up at my mine. If you pass three red hills you've gone too far. The rays of the setting sun shine on my gold. Climb above the mine

Suction Gully and North Buttress tower over Siphon Draw on the western escarpment of the Superstition Mountains.

Superstition Mountains

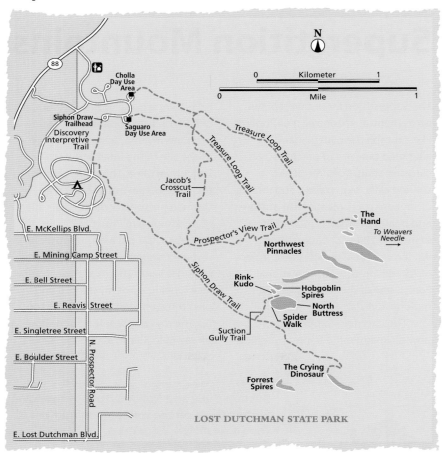

and you can see Weavers Needle." These few handed-down facts led to speculation, fantasy, and fiction. Fortune-seekers have searched tirelessly for the lost gold, and over fifty people have died or been killed looking for the lode.

The location of the mine and its supposed treasures have eluded everyone, and geologists say no gold exists in the Superstition's volcanic dust and ashes. Many historians believe the lost mine is a hidden cache of Spanish gold, possibly deposited in the 1840s by Don Miguel Peralta and his men after being attacked by Apaches. Another theory says Walz concocted his Superstition

mine story to cover a gold-laundering operation for high-graders at Wickenburg's Vulture Mine.

The Superstition Mountains were forged by volcanism between 15 and 24 million years ago. Most of the climbing occurs on two types of rock—intrusive, igneous dikes and necks, like Weavers Needle and The Hand, and tuff canyon walls. The tuff, deposited as volcanic ash, is generally soft. The surface, however, is often case-hardened and forms a sturdy surface for climbing. Vertical cracks were formed by fractures in the hardening rock, while softer pumice eroded into pockets and holes. Rock climbers find climbing routes here on towers, buttes, buttresses, and cliffs. Hundreds of technical routes, both sport and traditional lines, ascend many of the range's crags.

When climbing here, follow Leave No Trace rules. Dogs must be leashed. Pack out all trash. Dispose of human waste at least 300 feet from all water sources, including dry washes. It's best to carry out your toilet paper in a plastic baggie. If that is not possible, then burn it rather than burying it under a rock. Follow existing trails and paths whenever possible. All of the described crags have trails to their bases. Take the time to find and use them to avoid damaging desert plants. If you do hike cross-country, try to follow drainages or slickrock areas.

Many dangers are found in the Superstitions, including loose rock. Wear a helmet to protect yourself from falling rocks when climbing and belaying. Descents can be hazardous, with loose rock, cacti, and hazardous drop-offs. Some descents are by rappel. Carry extra webbing to replace worn and desiccated rappel slings.

All of the described routes are in Tonto National Forest but are accessed from Lost Dutchman State Park via Apache Junction to the west. While it is possible to park in subdivisions and hike to the climbs, it's best to enter the park because the access trails are easier to find and follow.

Getting there: The Superstition Mountains and Lost Dutchman State Park are east of Phoenix. To reach the climbing area, drive east from Phoenix on US 60 (Superstition Freeway) to Apache Junction. Take exit 196 onto South Idaho Road and drive north for 2.2 miles to North Apache Trail. Turn right onto North Apache Trail and drive northeast for 4.6 miles to a marked right turn for Lost Dutchman State Park (GPS: 33.464371 N / -111.482065 W). Turn right, enter the park, and drive 0.1 mile to the ranger station.

The climbing sites on the western escarpment of the Supes are reached from three trailhead areas on a dead-end spur road that begins past the ranger station. From the station, drive

0.2 mile to a right turn to the park campground; continue straight and drive 0.2 mile to Cholla Day Use Area on the left (not the best parking area to access the trails). Continue on the road another 0.1 mile to Saguaro Day Use Area on the left (GPS: 33.459280 N / -111.478170 W). This is the best place to park to hike to The Hand and the Northwest Pinnacles. Restrooms, water, and picnic tables are available. Drive another 0.1 mile to the Siphon Draw Trailhead and parking lot (GPS: 33.459541 N / -111.479746 W) at the end of the road. This is the best place to park to hike to Hobgoblin Spires, North Buttress, and The Crying Dinosaur.

Climbing Weavers Needle

Weavers Needle, a 4,553-foot-high butte, was the first technical climb established in the Superstitions. Apache or Pima Indians, probably wearing 5.10 Moccasyms, probably scrambled to the summit of the "Finger of God" centuries ago, although no trace of a Native American ascent has been found. Most early explorers looked at the peak as a landmark to begin their search for Jacob Walz's lost gold mine.

No one knows who did the first ascent, but a 1949 article in *Boy's Life* recounts the Kachinas climbing the Needle on Thanksgiving 1948. They believed they had made the fourth ascent. Now Weavers Needle, named for pioneer trapper and mountain man Pauline Weaver, is the most popular climb in the range, with a couple hundred people lining up each year to ascend the popular West Chimney (5.0) to the summit.

In the 1960s a group of Arizona Mountaineering Club members, including the legendary desert climber Bill Forrest, began pioneering routes on other towers and cliffs in the Supes. Notable ascents included Razor's Edge on The Hand by Bill Forrest, Key Punches, and Gary Garbert in 1965 and the Regular Route on The Crying Dinosaur by Forrest and Garbert in 1966.

A climber enjoys easy climbing on the first pitch of Razor's Edge on The Hand. LOGAN BERNDT

NORTHWEST PINNACLES

This spectacular collection of towers sits on the northwest side of the immense escarpment that forms the west end of the Superstition Mountains. The Hand, also called The Praying Hands, is a prominent, freestanding spire that stands by itself to the left of the main cliffs. The Tower and The Prong are between The Hand and the main cliffs, while The Iceberg sits on a ridge on the north side of the cliffs and east of The Hand.

The Hand

The Hand, a 150-foot-high pinnacle on the northwest side of the escarpment, offers the best and most popular spire route in the Superstitions. Large parties are not recommended on this route.

Getting there: Start at a trailhead on the east side of the Saguaro Day Use parking lot (GPS: 33.459562 N / -111.477810 W). Hike east on Treasure Loop Trail (#56), along the sloping bajada on the west side of the Superstitions. The spire is visible as you hike. The trail leaves the park and enters the national forest at less than 0.1 mile. It crosses Jacob's Crosscut Trail at 0.3 mile and then steadily climbs to a junction with Prospector's View Trail (#57) at 1 mile. Go left at the junction and hike less than 0.2 mile to a right turn onto a narrow climber's trail that heads northeast uphill for 0.3 mile to the base of The Hand route (GPS: 33.452447 N / -111.459166 W). Allow 45 minutes to hike the 1.8 miles from car to cliff.

1. Razor's Edge (5.6) 3 pitches. Begin below a gully on the southeast side of the spire. **Pitch 1:** Climb the gully (4th class) to a bolt anchor at a skyline notch between The Hand and The Thumb (the smaller pinnacle to the east). **Pitch 2:** Work up the left side of the ridge past a fixed piton and three bolts to a 2-bolt belay anchor on Chicken Ledge. **Pitch 3:** Continue up the airy ridge (5.6) past four bolts and two fixed pins to the summit anchors.

Descent: Make a two-rope, 150-foot rappel from summit bolts down the south face to the ground. **Rack:** Medium to large cams and nuts, plus two ropes.

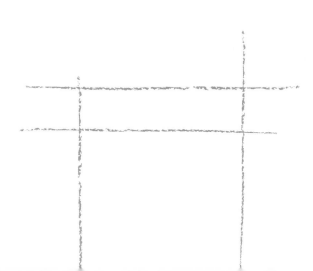

Hobgoblin Spires

The Hobgoblin Spires are several pinnacles that dominate the north wall of Suction Gully, the first side canyon left of Siphon Draw's obvious canyon. The spires are inconspicuous from many directions and blend into the high wall behind them. They are best seen from the amphitheater at the top of Suction Gully.

Getting there: Reach the pinnacles by starting at Siphon Draw Trailhead in Lost Dutchman State Park. Restrooms and water are at the parking lot. From the trailhead (GPS: 33.459374 N / -111.480019 W) on the southwest side of the parking area, hike south on the Discovery Interpretive Trail. At 0.2 mile, keep left past the hiker and biker campsites and reach Siphon Draw Trail (#53) at 0.25 mile. Go left on Siphon Draw Trail and cross the park boundary after almost 0.2 mile. Continue hiking steadily uphill, passing Jacob's Crosscut Trail (#58) at 0.3 mile and a left turn to Palmer Mine at 0.7 mile. After hiking 0.9 mile, look for a left turn onto a rough climber's trail that heads north up the right side of a gravel draw that drains out of the gully above (GPS: 33.445346 N / -111.467733W). Hike 0.2 mile up the steep path to the entrance to Suction Gully. Rink-Kudo is left of the entrance, and Spider Walk ascends the high buttress on the right. The Hobgoblin Spires are on the upper left side of the gully. Reach them by scrambling up the steep, boulder-filled gully into an amphitheater. The spires form the north wall. Allow about 1 hour from car to cliff.

2. Rink-Kudo (II 5.7 R) 4 pitches. A 450-foot route up the west side of the Hobgoblin Spires. The route ascends crack systems on the wall left of the entrance to Suction Gully. Watch for loose rock and wear helmets. Begin on the right side of the face at a left-angling crack system. **Pitch 1:** Work up double cracks until it's possible to step left (5.7) into the left-hand crack. Follow the crack up left to a narrow ledge 25 feet up. Continue up the crack in a thin, right-facing corner and behind a finger to a belay ledge. **Pitch 2:** From the middle of the ledge, climb a left-leaning crack system past a white spot. Squeeze through a hole at the top of the crack and move left to a tied-off belay boulder on a ledge beneath a chimney. **Pitch 3:** Work left and climb into the chimney for 80 feet to a belay stance at an obvious traverse to the left. **Pitch 4:** Traverse left on loose rock around a corner, then follow cracks and corners (5.7) up good rock to a false summit. Scramble east to a bouldering move onto the summit. 150 feet. Pro is sparse and hard to find on this pitch.

Descent: Downclimb south and east from the summit to a notch between a small pinnacle and the main wall. Use a belay on this exposed downclimb. Locate a tree

Downclimb east
to rappels

Hole

2

Pitch 4

XX

XX

XX

Suction
Gully

6

The rock on this variation is more solid.

Descent: Make four double-rope rappels down the route using the 2-bolt anchors at each stance. The rappel from The Eye is from a tied-off block. **Rack:** Wired nuts, medium to large cams, 2-foot slings, and two ropes.

The Crying Dinosaur

The Crying Dinosaur is a 200-foot-high tower high on the south side of Siphon Draw next to the main cliff. Siphon Draw is the deep canyon that slices through the western escarpment of the Superstition Mountains. Suction Gully and the North Buttress guard the left (north) side of the canyon's entrance, while the South Buttress and Forrest Spires flank the right (south) side.

The tower, which resembles a dinosaur with an open mouth from the trailhead, is hard to identify from a distance because it blends into the canyon walls. Before you leave the main trail, take time to locate the formation and scope out the surrounding terrain. The route, put up by Bill Forrest and Gary Garbert in 1966, ascends the north face and is visible from the trail. The line is often shaded, and sunlight rarely touches the tower's north face.

Getting there: Follow the directions above from Siphon Draw Trailhead to the turnoff to Suction Gully on Siphon Draw Trail (#53). From that turn, continue hiking east

up the main trail for another 0.5 mile (GPS: 33.442139 N / -111.460790 W) or until you are directly north of the obvious pinnacle to the south. Leave the main trail wherever it looks good, descend across the canyon floor, and hike up steep, brushy slopes past the west side of the tower to the base of a slope between it and the main wall to the south. Rack up and stash your packs here because the rappel ends on this side of the tower. Scramble around the east side of the tower to the base of the north face.

7. Regular Route (5.5) No topo. 3 pitches. Start near the middle of the north face below a crack system that leads up right to a huge flake pillar. **Pitch 1:** Work up a short groove and face (5.5) to an easy ramp. Follow the ramp up right to a bolt, then climb a chimney behind the flake pillar to an exposed 1-bolt belay stance on its right side. **Pitch 2:** Climb directly up to a hidden bolt and continue to a ledge/crack. Move up left along this crack to a 2-bolt belay stance. **Pitch 3:** Go up past a bolt and reach easier rock. Scamper to the summit and a 3-bolt belay anchor. The high point is just to the west.

Descent: Rappel 50 feet south from a 3-bolt summit anchor to an alcove ledge with anchors and a saguaro. Make a mostly free, double-rope rappel 150 feet down the south side of the formation. **Rack:** Medium to large cams and nuts, plus two ropes.

The Crying Dinosaur at the head of Siphon Draw is a classic Superstition climbing route.

WEAVERS NEEDLE

Weavers Needle, dominating the Superstition Range, is one of Arizona's most striking and famous landmarks. The 4,553-foot-high peak is climbed by an easy but potentially dangerous route to the summit. Don't underestimate the route or its objective dangers, including heat, lack of water, lack of protection and belay anchors, and other climbers. Avoid climbing the Needle on weekends in spring and fall—it can be really busy! Elevation gain from the trailhead is 3,400 vertical feet with about 600 feet of climbing terrain. Round-trip hiking distance is 8 miles.

Getting there: The Peralta Trailhead is the jumping-off point for Weavers Needle. From Phoenix, drive east on US 60 (Superstition Freeway). From Apache Junction, drive another 8 miles on US 60 to a well-marked left (north) turn onto Peralta Road (FR 77) between mileposts 204 and 205. Follow this dirt road for 8 miles to a dead end at the trailhead (GPS: 33.397417 N / -111.348044 W0). Peralta Trail (#102) goes up Peralta Canyon and over Fremont Saddle to the west side of Weavers Needle.

Begin at Peralta Trailhead and hike northwest for 2.25 miles on Peralta Trail to 3,766-foot-high Fremont Saddle (GPS: 33.415712 N / -111.364767 W). The saddle offers an excellent view of Weavers Needle. Continue on Peralta Trail into East Boulder Canyon to Pinyon Camp, a good camping spot. One mile north of Pinyon Camp (4 miles from Peralta Trailhead), leave the trail and hike east up a trail on steep talus to the base of a steep gully that lies between the higher north summit and the lower south summit (GPS: 33.432375 N / -111.371241 W). Work left into the gully below the west face of the south summit and climb the gully (3rd-class scrambling over rock steps) to the foot of the first pitch, about 150 feet below an obvious chockstone in a notch.

1. West Chimney (III 5.0) 4 pitches. The classic Supes route. **Pitch 1:** Climb 60 feet of 4th-class rock to a small ledge on the left wall of the gully. A pipe hammered into the rock offers protection. **Pitch 2:** Continue up poorly protected but easy 5th-class 5 rock to a chockstone. Here the leader has three choices. Crawl under the chockstone (5.0), climb left of the chockstone (5.4), or climb right of the chockstone (5.2). Belay from several rappel bolts atop the chockstone. Pitches 1 and 2 can be combined in a long lead. **Pitch 3:** From a notch, scramble 15 feet up a step (3rd-class 3) and continue up a gully with easy rock steps for about 300 feet to the southwest face of the final summit headwall. **Pitch 4:** Easy but exposed and dangerous climbing. There are no good anchors available at the bottom of the pitch. Use extreme caution. Climb a broken groove (4th class) up left for 40 feet and follow a juggy crack to a natural horn for an anchor belay. Scramble onto the summit for

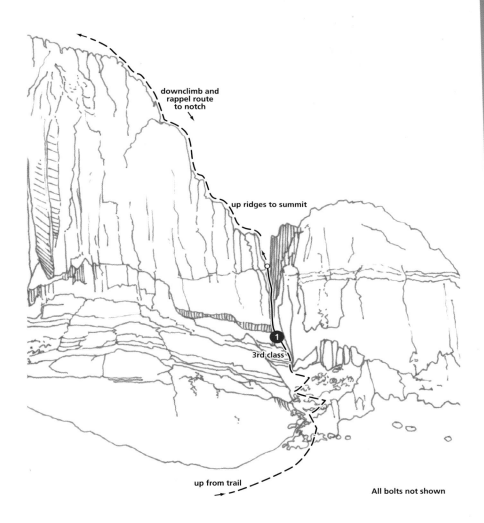

downclimb and
rappel route
to notch

up ridges to summit

3rd class

up from trail

All bolts not shown

spectacular 360-degree views.

Descent: Scramble down to bolt anchors south of the top of pitch 4. Rappel back to the gully and downclimb to the notch between the south and north summits. From bolt anchors atop the chockstone in the notch, make a long, two-rope rappel west to the base of pitch 1. **Rack:** Wired nuts and medium to large nuts and cams, plus extra runners, two ropes, and a helmet.

Pete Takeda leads Weak Sister, one of the best and longest climbs at The Pond.

Queen Creek Canyon

Queen Creek Canyon slices sharply through the southeastern edge of the Superstition Mountains east of Phoenix. The canyon, carved by Queen Creek and traced by US 60, is lined with compact cliffs, buttresses, pinnacles, and fins composed of pocketed volcanic ash.

The rock offers great climbing, with sinker pockets, shallow dishes, crisp edges, and positive holds. The rock is ash flow tuff that was deposited between 15 and 24 million years ago by violent volcanic eruptions. Much of the soft rock was hardened by heat and pressure. Queen Creek, like other welded tuff climbing areas, offers vertical faces for climbers.

The large number of bolted and trad routes at Queen Creek Canyon and surrounding areas, including Devil's Canyon, Oak Flat, and Apache Leap, make this Arizona's premier sport climbing area. The area offers almost 1,000 routes and over 2,000 boulder problems with a diversity of climbing experiences, from pocketed slabs and vertical crimpfests to overhanging jug hauls and technical testpieces. Traditional crack climbs are also found. Routes range in difficulty from 5.6 to 5.13, with most between 5.9 and 5.11, making Queen Creek an ideal destination. The area does, however, have lots of 5.12 and 5.13 routes, as well as a possible 5.14 on the big overhang. The Queen Creek Canyon crags are easily accessible, lining the highway corridor, making most approaches less than 10 minutes from car to cliff.

The described cliffs lie along US 60 and are the most accessible Queen Creek crags. Atlantis, a narrow canyon below the highway, is lined with moderate routes up to 80 feet long. The shady corridor is a perfect destination on warm days. The Pond, a long cliff band above the highway, has a generous selection of moderate classics.

Climbing is possible year-round, although summer days are usually hot, with highs reaching into the low 100s. Early summer mornings are best, when the temperatures are still cool. Atlantis is a good summer option. October through April are the best months for climbing. Sun or shade is easily found in the canyon. At an elevation of 3,600 feet, an occasional snowflake might fly in winter, but 60 degrees, clear, and no wind is normal.

**Picketpost Mountain
rises beyond Jim
Waugh climbing
The Soft Parade
at The Pond.**

Queen Creek Canyon

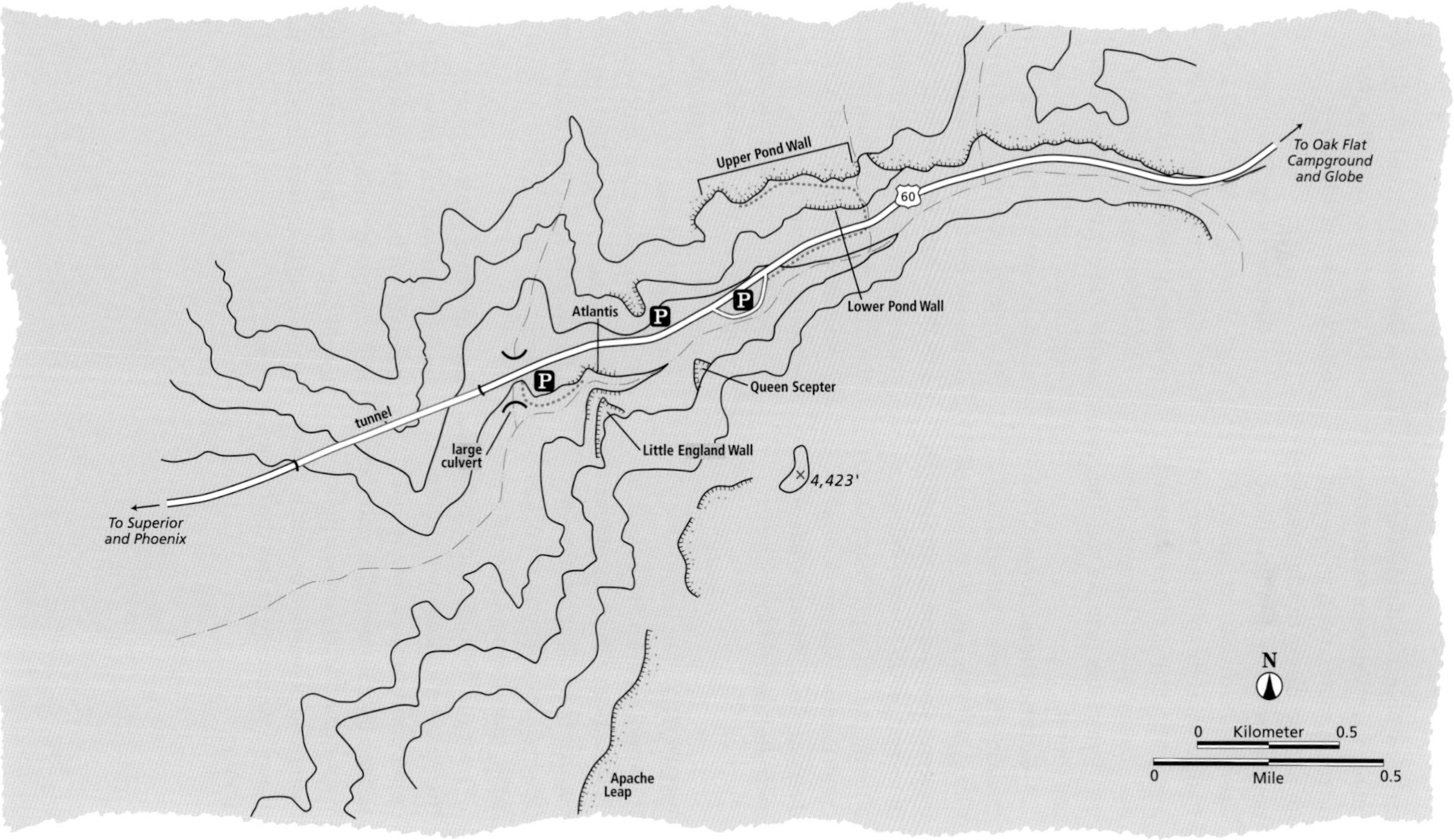

To Oak Flat
Campground
and Globe

Upper Pond Wall

Lower Pond Wall

60

Queen Scepter

Little England Wall

×4,423'

Atlantis

large
culvert

tunnel

Apache
Leap

To Superior
and Phoenix

N

0   Kilometer   0.5

0   0.5
Mile

Few objective dangers are found here. Watch for loose flakes on some routes. Keep an eye out for rattlesnakes in brushy areas and boulder fields. Be careful walking along and crossing the highway. Traffic travels through the canyon pretty fast. Many of the routes still have cold shut bolt hangers. Check these for cracks to make sure they are still sound.

Getting there: Queen Creek Canyon is between Superior and Globe, 60 miles east of Phoenix. US 60 traverses the canyon. From Superior, drive east on US 60 for 4 miles. Just after the tunnel, you'll reach Queen Creek Canyon. Specific access directions and parking areas are in each site's description.

THE POND

The Pond, on the hillside north of US 60, is one of the best and most popular sport climbing areas at Queen Creek Canyon. Lots of south-facing routes, ranging from 5.6 to 5.13, ascend the cliff bands and make The Pond an ideal winter crag. The upper pond, nestled among cliffs and fed by a 50-foot-high waterfall in spring and after rain, is a good swimming hole when it's hot. It's best to avoid swimming unless the creek is running.

Descent: Descent off all routes is by lowering or rappelling for established bolt anchors.

Getting there: Drive east from Superior on US 60 and park at the third pullout on the right past the tunnel (GPS: 33.308500 N / -111.070525 W). The pullout is on the south side of a rock island. Walk east along the south side of the highway on a trail that parallels the guardrail. At a bridge, drop down and pass under the bridge to the opposite side of the highway. Avoid crossing the highway. Traffic is fast, making the crossing a risky maneuver. Lower Pond Wall is the lower cliff band up left from the bridge.

To reach the upper tier, follow a climber's trail over bedrock right of the lower pond, a small water pocket that often dries up, and then climb up boulders and grooves with glued-in ladder rungs (3rd class) right of a cascade water flow to the upper pond.

Lower Pond Wall

Lower Pond Wall is the lower cliff band up left from the creek and the highway bridge. Hike up a short, rough trail from the creek to the base of the wall. Routes are listed left to right.

Upper Pond Walls

Bartuni Wall

Pocket Puzzle

Lower Pond Wall

Access up gully

Trail to The Pond

US 60

1. Return from the Ultimate Mormon Experience (5.12b) Recommended. Uphill from Rock Lobster. Start left of a right-angling chimney. Climb a steep, technical wall right of a blunt prow to crux moves. Finish up juggy holds to anchors just below the cliff top. 10 bolts to 2-bolt anchor.

2. Rock Lobster (5.10a) Fun climbing up a corner system to a pocketed face. 8 bolts to 2-bolt anchor.

3. Clueless (5.11c) Climb a couple faces to a ledge with a boulder. Finish up a prow. 9 bolts to 2-bolt anchor.

4. Ninja School (5.10d) Start up a ramp to a short face and ledge. Climb the left side of a steep triangular face to anchors. 9 bolts to 2-bolt anchor.

5. Liquid Sunshine (5.10c) Quality route. Begin below some boulders. Climb a boulder with a bolt, then step up left onto a ledge. Climb bulges on the triangular face to anchors on a high ledge. 6 bolts to 2-bolt anchor.

A 2-bolt anchor on a ledge above a chimney allows a quick 80-foot rappel from the Upper Pond cliffs down the Lower Pond Wall to the cliff base.

6. Noah's Ark (5.10c) Climb corners to a steep prow. 7 bolts to 2-bolt anchor.

7. Taking It to the Street (5.9) Good moderate route up the slabby right side of the wall. 9 bolts to 2-bolt anchor.

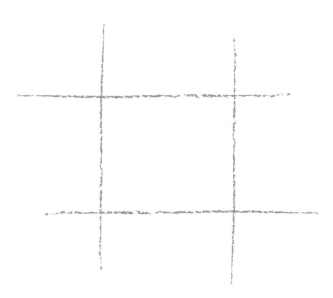

Rappel from
upper cliffs
80′ ↓ XX

Upper Pond Wall

The Upper Pond Wall is a low band of cliffs that surround the upper pond. Routes are listed right to left. Reach the first four routes by scrambling up right from the pond to a short, southeast-facing cliff.

8. Beer and Dead Animals (5.9) A good, short, pocketed line on the right side of the wall. 2 bolts to 2-bolt anchor.

9. El Gato Grande D'Amore (5.12a) Climb thin holds on the right side of an obvious white streak. Find a bolt at the lip of a roof at the top. 4 bolts to 2-bolt anchor.

10. Crazy Fingers (5.11c) Excellent. Climb the left side of a wide white streak to a final roof with a bolt at its lip. 5 bolts to 2-bolt anchor. Stick-clip the first bolt.

11. Natural Wonder (5.8) A good hand to off-width crack left of Crazy Fingers.

Descent: Rappel from Crazy Fingers's anchors. **Rack:** Medium to large cams and large Camalots.

The next two routes begin on a large ledge overlooking the pond, a deep water-filled pothole tucked into the cliffs. Scramble up the right-hand trail and traverse left across an obvious ledge to a 2-bolt belay stance. No topos.

12. Interloper (5.11b/c) Belay from bolts on the left side of the ledge. Work up overhanging rock left of the large, angled roof above the belay. Pull pockets up the steep wall, over a bulge, and to a vertical finish. 8 bolts to 2-bolt anchor.

13. Inner Basin (5.10c) Start from the 2-bolt belay stance for Interloper. Traverse left on the ledge and pull onto a small stance with a bush below a crack system. Climb directly up the vertical face above to anchors. 5 bolts to 2-bolt belay.

There are two routes just left of Inner Basin and right of the pour-off groove. Big Legged Woman (5.10b) is a 5-bolt route reached by rapping from the top to its 2-bolt anchor, and Drowning (5.10a), a slippery 5-bolt route up water-polished rock. Both start from hanging belays above the water.

The following routes are left of the pond. Follow a trail past the pond to the cliff's base. Routes are listed right to left from the pond.

14. Dead Pool (5.9) Scramble up left from the pond and climb a short face with two bolts onto a ledge with a 2-bolt belay anchor. Move up right and then up a rounded prow past eight more bolts. 10 bolts to 2-bolt anchor.

15. Easy Pool (5.7+) Start on the ledge with the bolt anchor (same as Dead Pool). Fun, well-protected moves climb lots of pockets up the middle of the face. 9 bolts to 2-bolt anchor.

16. Date Rape (5.7 R) Start on the same ledge as Dead Pool. Climb up left from the belay ledge to a bolt below a horizontal break. Continue up the left side of the face. 70 feet. 4 bolts to 2-bolt anchor.

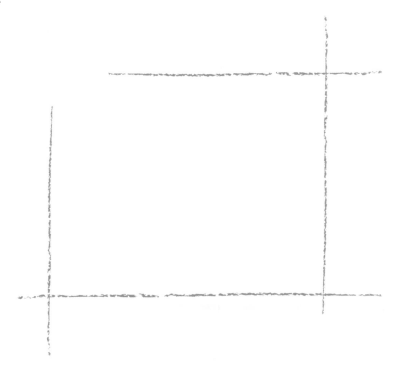

17. Mistaken Identity (5.12b) Begin left of Date Rape on the far right side of an overhanging wall. Climb up right on an easy ramp past a bolt to a ledge. Pull up the overhanging face left of a chimney. 7 bolts to 2-bolt anchor.

18. Hot House (5.12c) Same start as Mistaken Identity. From the ledge, climb directly up the steep face. 7 bolts to 2-bolt anchor.

19. Hot Line (5.12d) Same start as Mistaken Identity and Hot House. From the left side of the ledge, follow bolts up a black streak to a bulge finish. 6 bolts to 2-bolt anchor.

20. Death Row (5.12d) Classic climbing but a lot of drilled holds. Swing up the overhanging wall left of an angling crack and black streak using pockets and crimps to anchors on the lip. 6 bolts to 2-bolt anchor.

21. Desert Devil (5.13a) Good climbing up the middle of The Pond's steepest face. Climb the middle of the steep wall with thin gastons and a hard crux at the last move. 7 bolts to 2-bolt anchor.

22. The Emerald (5.13b) Follow a line of bolts up left to anchors over the lip. 7 bolts to 2-bolt anchor.

23. Project (5.14?) Up the left side of the overhanging wall to a steep, bulgy finish. 7 bolts to 2-bolt anchor.

24. Out on Parole (5.10c) Good and pumpy. Start below the far left side of the overhanging wall and right of a crack. Work up the left side of the wall to a pocketed bulge. Finish up an overhanging headwall. 5 bolts to 2-bolt anchor.

25. Pompasfuc (5.12b) Variation to Out on Parole. Move out right at the third bolt and finish with pumpy pockets up overhanging rock. 5 bolts to 2-bolt anchor.

26. Weak Sister (5.10a) Popular and pleasant. Begin right of a chimney cleft. Climb crux crimps up a slab past two bolts to a left-angling crack, or stem up the shallow chimney to the left for an easier start. Stand up high and make a delicate step right to the third bolt. Move left over a bulge and motor up the steep slab to anchors at the upper horizontal break. 6 bolts to 2-bolt anchor.

A climber on Weak Sister
at The Pond.

The next three routes are on two short walls up left of the overhanging wall.

27. Behind Bars (5.10a) On the low buttress left of Weak Sister. "Ugly route!" says local author Marty Karabin. Pockets and edges to anchors right of a yucca on top of the cliff. 25 feet. 3 bolts to 2-bolt anchor.

28. The Warden (5.10b) On the flat face left of Behind Bars. Climb pockets up the vertical face to anchors at the rock's high point. 4 bolts to 2-bolt anchor.

29. Kitty Litter (5.9) Short route up the face left of The Warden. 4 bolts to 2-bolt anchor.

Upper Pond West

To reach this cliff band, continue hiking uphill along a trail left (west) from the pond. Past The Warden, the trail steps around an airy corner to an upper cliff. Routes are listed right to left above the trail.

30. Pony Express (5.5) Fun and easy. Climb pockets up a short face. 4 bolts to 2-bolt anchor.

31. Leave Your Money on the Dresser (5.10b) Short, steep route up a face left of Pony Express. 3 bolts to 2-bolt anchor.

32. Cowgirl (5.9) Climb a short 35-foot route just right of Cowboy. 4 bolts to 2-bolt anchor.

33. Cowboy (5.10a) On a southeast-facing wall. Begin on boulders around a corner right of and above a juniper at the cliff base. Climb a pocketed slab with a light streak to a 3-bolt headwall. The first bolt is reached by easy but runout climbing up a ramp slab. 3 bolts to 2-bolt anchor.

34. Pocket Warmer (5.6) Good for beginners or a first lead. Up a short buttress left of Cowboy. Climb pockets past bolts to a 2-bolt anchor.

The next six routes are on a clean, southeast-facing panel of rock. All of them offer similar pocket climbing.

35. Main Squeeze (5.11a) Sustained pocket pulling up the right side of a clean panel. 5 bolts to 2-bolt anchor.

36. Pocket Pow-Wow (5.10b) Recommended and fun. The right route on the steep, southeast-facing panel. A bouldery start to the first bolt, then up pockets and edges to an anchor below a ledge. 5 bolts to 2-bolt anchor.

37. Space Hog (5.10c) Chase crimps and pockets up the vertical face to a high rest. Finish up slightly overhanging rock. 65 feet. 8 bolts to 2-bolt anchor.

38. Pocket Party (5.10b) Excellent. Just left of Space Hog on the left side of the face. Fun and pumpy climbing leads up a long, pocketed face to anchors at the top of the cliff. 7 bolts to 2-bolt anchor.

39. Pocket Pulling Pansies (5.10b) Climb the far left edge of the vertical panel, passing a couple of left-angling cracks to a steep finish. 6 bolts to 2-bolt anchor.

40. Rocky Horror Picture Show (5.10d) Start just left of Pocket Pulling Pansies. Climb steep, bouldery rock past a roof. Follow bolts up left and pull past an overhang to a steep finish. 10 bolts to 2-bolt anchor.

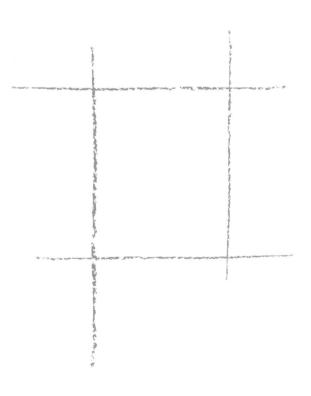

41. Just Can't Get Any (5.12b) Located on an overhanging, triangular face. Pull over a big roof and pump it up to anchors at the lip. Some chipped holds. 3 bolts to 2-bolt anchor.

The next three routes are on the left side of the buttress left of the Pocket Party wall. The first route climbs over a big roof.

42. Arête Horizon (5.10a) Excellent route! Begin just left of Just Can't Get Any. Climb a crux bouldery start on the left side of a roof to great pockets on a blunt arête. Catch a good rest at a stance, then finish up a steep headwall to high anchors. 9 bolts to 2-bolt anchor.

43. Pocket Puzzle (5.10a) Superb, excellent, fun, awesome! The west-facing, vertical wall left around the corner from Just Can't Get Any. Work up the steep, sustained, pocketed face to a break and rest, then continue over the bulge above to a finishing slab. 70 feet. 8 bolts to 2-bolt anchor.

44. Adventure Quest (5.8) Climb a couple short faces to a stance, then up a narrow rib between cracks to anchors. 8 bolts to 2-bolt anchor.

A climber leads Pocket Puzzle, one of the best routes at The Pond.

Bartuni Wall

The following routes ascend the Bartuni Wall, a clean, south-facing panel of pocketed rock.

45. The Soft Parade (5.11a) Classic Queen Creek climb. The right side of the south-facing wall left of a big, left-facing dihedral and Adventure Quest. Follow a line of bolts up right to anchors above a finishing bulge. 85 feet. 10 bolts to 2-bolt anchor.

46. Bartuni (5.11b) 10 feet left of The Soft Parade. Climb a thin slab to the first bolt. Grab small crimps, edges, and pockets to a tricky, final headwall. 90 feet. 10 bolts to 2-bolt anchor. Use a 200-foot (60-meter) rope.

47. Blisters in the Sun (5.12a) Start 6 feet left of Bartuni. Climb crimps, edges, and pockets directly up a steep wall to anchors above a slanting break. 10 bolts to 2-bolt anchor.

48. Time Share (5.12a) Thin climbing on loose, white rock with pockets and flexible flakes. Crimp and edge up the left side of the face to anchors at the cliff top. 8 bolts to 2-bolt anchor.

49. Mona Lisa (5.11b) Begin on the left side of the wall below a left-angling crack system. A bouldery start leads to a shallow, open corner that goes up left. Pull a thin upper bulge with a crack to anchors at a horizontal crack. 9 bolts to 2-bolt anchor.

50. Adamantasaurus Flacciphallicus Phd

(5.11a) No topo. Far left side of Bartuni Wall. Work up a roof or traverse in from the left, then climb a steep, tricky wall. Continue on sustained moves to high anchors. 11 bolts to 2-bolt anchor. 95 feet. Use a 200-foot (60-meter) rope. Stick-clip the first bolt.

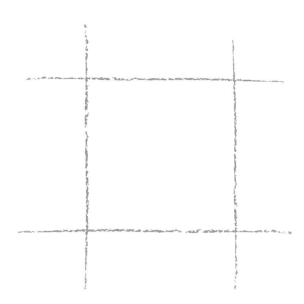

The next route is around the edge of the blunt prow on the left side of Bartuni Wall.

51. The Big Weld Show (5.11a) No topo. Good climbing up a steep, pocketed wall. Climb a short corner then up the crux overhanging face. Above, climb bulges and steep rock. 90 feet. 11 bolts to 2-bolt anchor.

Step left from The Big Weld Show to a south-facing panel split by a couple of intermittent crack systems.

52. Close Call (5.10c) The face left of a big, left-facing dihedral. Climb good rock to a broken section, then finish up a steep headwall. 9 bolts to 2-bolt anchor.

53. Nothing Lasts Forever (5.10d) Marty Karabin calls this an "awesome, classic route!" Left from Close Call. Begin right of a large boulder. Climb

a blunt prow past three bolts to a sloping ledge. Step up left and work up steep, vertical rock to anchors above the last break. 9 bolts to 2-bolt anchor. Use a 200-foot (60-meter) rope.

54. In Seam (5.10c) Start left of a small pillar below a seam crack. Climb the seam, clipping bolts on the left to a crux at a horizontal crack. 8 bolts to 2-bolt anchor.

55. Casting Shadows (5.11b) Recommended. Start left of In Seam and right of a deep chimney. Climb pockets and thin edges up a vertical face. Crux is one-finger pockets above the second bolt. 7 bolts to 2-bolt anchor.

56. The Casting Couch (5.9) Climb pockets and edges up the left edge of the face next to a chimney. 9 bolts to 2-bolt anchor.

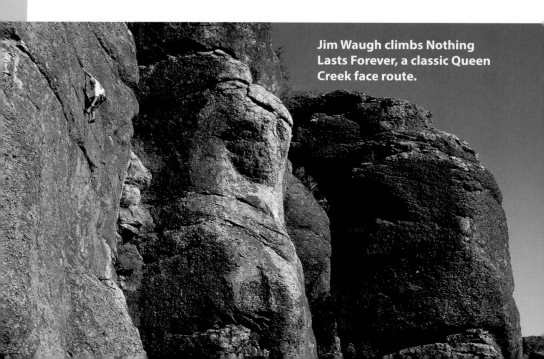

Jim Waugh climbs Nothing Lasts Forever, a classic Queen Creek face route.

The next routes are around a broken buttress from The Casting Couch and the deep chimney.

57. God Save the Ta-Tas (5.8) Begin about 10 feet right of a deep crack system. A tricky start leads to easier face climbing. 5 bolts to 2-bolt anchor.

58. Christmas Chocolate (5.7) Good beginner climb. Begin just right of the deep crack. Fun moves lead up the face right of the crack. 5 bolts to 2-bolt anchor.

59. Follow Your Heart (5.8) Fun pocket route. Start left of the crack. Climb past a bolt just above a roof, then grab good pockets to a chain anchor at the top. 5 bolts to 2-bolt anchor.

60. Sappy Love Song (5.8) On the left side of the panel. Fun pocket pulling leads up the steep face to anchors on the cliff top. It's a bit runout above the third bolt. 4 bolts to 2-bolt anchor.

61. Fat Boy Goes to the Pond (5.6) One of the easier climbs. The route climbs the short buttress left of Sappy Love Song and a deep chimney. Climb the slabby prow of a narrow pillar to anchors on a small ledge. 3 bolts to 2-bolt anchor.

To reach the next routes, walk left and scramble over boulders to the cliff tier behind and to the north. The first two routes are on the smooth,

south-facing wall on the right side. The other routes are to the left.

62. Endomorph Man (5.12c) Hard, thin moves on the right side of the wall. Climb shallow pockets and small edges past four bolts, then angle up left to a final slab and anchors at the cliff top. 5 bolts to 2-bolt anchor.

63. Loc-Tite (5.11d) Great route on the left side of the panel. Pick pockets and edges up the steep wall right of a right-facing dihedral. 6 bolts to 2-bolt anchor.

64. Chutes and Ladders (5.7) Good warmup route left of a right-facing dihedral. Climb a crack system and then a ridge. 6 bolts to 2-bolt anchor.

65. Great Short Route (5.9) Climb with pockets and edges up a short face left of Chutes and Ladders. 4 bolts to 2-bolt anchor.

66. Nothing's Right (5.7) Walk left and downhill from Great Short Route to a pocketed face. A boulder-problem start leads to fun climbing up the right side of the steep, pocketed slab. 5 bolts to 2-bolt anchor.

67. Nothing's Left (5.8) Start 6 feet left of Nothing's Right. More fun climbing up the left side of the face. 5 bolts to 2-bolt anchor.

68. Nothing Shocking (5.8) No topo. Climb a fun, slabby arête left of Nothing's Left. Start direct or traverse

in from the left (5.7). 5 bolts to 2-bolt anchor.

69. Nothing Becomes Her (5.9) No topo. Do a tricky start, then climb easier rock on the west-facing wall left of the arête. 5 bolts to 2-bolt anchor.

70. Nothing to It (5.10c) Scramble west from Nothing Becomes Her past a small outcrop to the next buttress. Start left of a crack and climb a steep, pocketed face. 45 feet. 5 bolts to 2-bolt anchor.

71. Next to Nothing (5.5) Continue west on the trail to the next buttress right of a big dihedral. Fun pockets up the easy slab. 4 bolts to 2-bolt anchor.

72. Nothing's There (5.11d) On the right side of a streaked face, left of a diagonal crack, and up a large, right-facing dihedral. Climb past the diagonal crack, then up the steep, edgy wall. 5 bolts to 2-bolt anchor below a ledge.

73. Is Nothing Sacred (5.11b/c) Climb directly up the center of the wall with a low crux and good upper pockets. 5 bolts to 2-bolt anchor.

74. Nothing but Air (5.11d) The left side of the wall. Pull up a series of angling seams and breaks to anchors. 5 bolts to 2-bolt anchor.

75. Princess Jordini and Her Magic Flute (5.5) No topo. An easy and fun pocketed slab on the far left side of The Pond. 3 bolts to 2-bolt anchor.

15. Shark Attack (5.12a) Good climbing with big jugs between long moves on this steep, overhanging bulge on the far right side of the cliff. 40 feet. 3 bolts to 2-bolt anchor. All bolts not shown on topo.

South Atlantis

South Atlantis is the cliff on the south side of the creek. Routes are listed left to right (east to west). The first route, Diaper Rash, is 50 feet upstream to the east from the concrete dam on the left side of a boulder-filled gully.

16. Diaper Rash (5.10a) No topo. Begin off boulders above the creek bed on the left side of the obvious gully. Face climb just left of a crack system to a horizontal break/ledge. Continue over a bulge to a headwall finish. 5 bolts to 2-bolt anchor.

17. U.S. Senators Are Space Aliens (5.11a) East of the top of the dam on the right side of the gully. Climb a blunt prow to a sloping ledge. Move over bulges to anchors. 6 bolts to 2-bolt anchor.

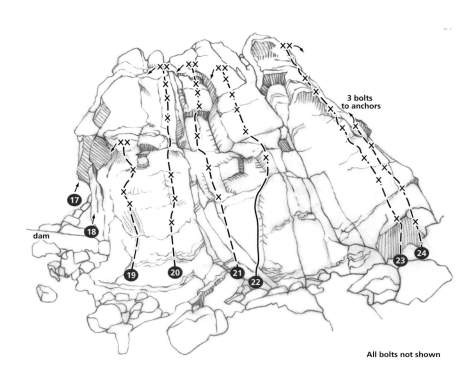

3 bolts to anchors

dam

All bolts not shown

18. Project (A crack project) Begin from the top of the dam. Climb a finger crack up the overhanging wall and move right to a wide crack finish. 2 bolts to 2-bolt anchor. **Rack:** Selection of cams.

19. Unknown (5.12) Start 10 feet right of the dam base below an overhanging wall. Crank the steep wall with small crimps to a bulge, then work out right with layback flakes to anchors above the lip. 40 feet. 3 bolts to 2-bolt anchor.

20. Duck and Cover (5.11d) Begin just right of Unknown and left of a broken, double crack system. Move over a bulge to a pocketed face and a sloping rest shelf. Edge up the vertical wall above to anchors beneath a nose. 6 bolts to 2-bolt anchor.

21. Shoot First, Ask Later (5.11d) Recommended classic. Right of a double crack system. Climb broken rock to a sloping ledge. Head up the pocketed face right of a chimney to a slab finish. 7 bolts to 2-bolt anchor. All bolts not shown on topo.

22. Grumpy After Eight (5.10a) Great climbing that will make you smile! Begin by moving up a right-angling crack and broken face for 20 feet to a large ledge. Continue up the steep, pocketed face right of a chimney to a final slab. 6 bolts to 2-bolt anchor. All bolts not shown on topo.

23. KGB (5.10b) 40 feet right of Grumpy After Eight on the left side of a buttress. Thin face climbing leads past four bolts to a small overhang. Pull onto the upper slab and move up right to a second roof. Pull the roof to a bulging finish. 7 bolts to 2-bolt anchor.

24. Giggling Marlin (5.9) Laughable entertainment all the way. 8 feet right of KGB. Good face moves lead to a small, left-facing corner. Climb a corner crack to a right-facing corner capped by a roof. A slab leads to an upper crack/groove and anchors. 8 bolts to 3-bolt anchor.

25. Bunny Slope (5.8) 15 feet right of Giggling Marlin. Fun moderate line. Climb pockets for 15 feet to the first bolt. Go right into a short crack to a spacious, sloping ledge. Step right on the ledge and climb the face and bulges past a couple of breaks to a final bulging prow. At the fourth bolt move left to cracks, then back right above to keep the grade 5.8; otherwise the face moves are 5.11. 6 bolts to 2-bolt anchor.

Martha Morris belays Jim Waugh on the The Soft Parade, at the Upper Pond Wall.

Traffic whizzes below while climbers take turns on Pocket Puzzle.

27 uphill in gully

All bolts not shown

26. Sir Charles (5.10a) Begin on the outside (west) face of a buttress 20 feet right of some old cables. Climb an easy, broken chimney to a large ledge. Climb the right side of the vertical face above to anchors. 5 bolts to 2-bolt anchor.

27. Mondo Freako (5.7) No topo. Scramble up right from Sir Charles to the base of a slab left of a gully. Fun pocket moves lead up the left side of the slab. 3 bolts to 2-bolt anchor.

QUEEN SCEPTER

This spectacular, semidetached pinnacle is on the slope south of the highway and above the creek. Two excellent routes ascend the obvious, steep west face.

Getting there: Approach Queen Scepter by parking at the second pullout on the south side of the highway east of the tunnel. Drop down to the creek and scramble up a climber's path to the base of the west face. Routes are listed left to right, or counterclockwise from the west face.

1. Queen of Hearts (5.12b/c) Long pitch up the left side of the tiered west face. Work up and over several roofs to anchors just below the top. 120 feet. 15 bolts to 2-bolt anchor.

Descent: Make two single-rope rappels down Queen Scepter.

2. Queen Scepter (5.12a) Sport line up the west face. 110 feet. 15 bolts to 2-bolt anchor.

Descent: Make two single-rope rappels from two sets of anchors.

3. King of Fools (5.11d) No topo. On the north side of the rock. Hard face moves up and over a roof. 10 bolts to 2-bolt anchor.

4. Whistling Idiot (5.10b) No topo. On the east face. 4 bolts to 2-bolt anchor.

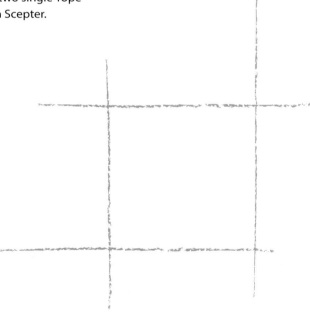

Last Light at the McDowell Mountains is a perfect winter climb.

Appendix

Government Agencies

Camelback Mountain—Echo Canyon
Recreation Area
5700 N. Echo Canyon Pkwy.
Phoenix, AZ 85018
Ranger office: (602) 261-8318
www.phoenix.gov/parks/trails/
locations/camelback-mountain

Lost Dutchman State Park
6109 N. Apache Trail
Apache Junction, AZ 85119
(480) 982-4485
azstateparks.com/Parks/LODU/

McDowell Sonoran Preserve
7447 E. Indian School Rd., #300
Scottsdale, AZ 85251
(480) 312-7013

Pinnacle Peak Park
26802 N. 102nd Way
Scottsdale, AZ 85262
(480) 312-0990
www.scottsdaleaz.gov/parks/
pinnacle-peak-park

Tonto National Forest
2325 E. McDowell Rd.
Phoenix, AZ 85006
(602) 225-5200
www.fs.usda.gov/tonto/

Climbing Shops, Gyms, and Guide Services

360 Adventures
(480) 722-0360
www.360-adventures.com/
arizona-rock-climbing

Ape Index Rock Climbing Gym
9700 N. 91st Ave.
Peoria, AZ 85345
(623) 242-9164
www.apeindex.net

Arizona Climbing and Adventure
School
P.O. Box 3094
Carefree, AZ 85377
(480) 363-2390
climbingschool.com

Arizona Hiking Shack
3244 E. Thomas Rd.
Phoenix, AZ 85018
(602) 944-7723
www.hikingshack.com

AZ on the Rocks
16447 N. 91st St., #105
Scottsdale, AZ 85260
(480) 502-9777
www.azontherocks.com

ClimbMax Climbing Gym
1330 W. Auto Dr., Ste. 108
Tempe, AZ 85284
(480) 626-7755
www.climbmaxclimbinggym.com

Focus Climbing Center
2150 W. Broadway Rd., #103
Mesa, AZ 85202
(480) 718-5258
focusclimbingcenter.com

Front Range Climbing
Company—Arizona
(719) 532-5822
www.frontrangeclimbing.com

Phoenix Rock Gym
1353 E. University Dr.
Tempe, AZ 85281
(480) 921-8322
phoenixrockgym.com

REI
12634 N. Paradise Village Pkwy.
Phoenix, AZ 85032
(602) 996-5400
www.rei.com/stores/paradise-valley
.html

REI
1405 W. Southern Ave.
Tempe, AZ 85282
(480) 967-5494
www.rei.com/stores/tempe.html

Index

About the Author

Stewart M. Green is a lifelong climber as well as a professional writer and photographer. He is the author of *Best Climbs Moab, Rock Climbing Colorado, Rock Climbing New England, Rock Climbing Utah, Scenic Routes and Byways California's Pacific Coast*, and many other FalconGuides. He also writes and photographs for publications, including *Alpinist, Climbing*, and *Rock and Ice*. Stewart lives in Colorado, where he is also a Senior Climbing Guide for Front Range Climbing Company.

PROTECTING CLIMBING **ACCESS** SINCE 1991